Your U.S. Citizenship Guide

What You Need to Know to Pass Your U.S. Citizenship Test

With Companion CD-ROM

By Anita Biase

YOUR U.S. CITIZENSHIP GUIDE: WHAT YOU NEED TO KNOW TO PASS YOUR U.S. CITIZENSHIP TEST — WITH COMPANION CD-ROM

Copyright © 2009 by Atlantic Publishing Group, Inc.
1405 SW 6th Ave. • Ocala, Florida 34471 • 800-814-1132 • 352-622-1875–Fax
Web site: www.atlantic-pub.com • E-mail: sales@atlantic-pub.com
SAN Number: 268-1250

ISBN-13: 978-1-60138-135-4   ISBN-10: 1-60138-135-2

Library of Congress Cataloging-in-Publication Data

Biase, Anita, 1946-
Your U.S. citizenship guide : what you need to know to pass your U.S. citizenship test, with companion CD-ROM / by Anita Biase.
    p. cm.
Includes bibliographical references and index.
ISBN-13: 978-1-60138-135-4 (alk. paper)
ISBN-10: 1-60138-135-2 (alk. paper)
1. Naturalization--United States. 2. Citizenship--United States. 3. Emigration and immigration law--United States. I. Title.

KF4710.B53 2008
342.7308'3--dc22
                            2008005886

COVER DESIGN: Meg Buchner • megadesn@mchsi.com

Printed in the United States

Printed on Recycled Paper

We recently lost our beloved pet "Bear," who was not only
our best and dearest friend but also the "Vice President of
Sunshine" here at Atlantic Publishing. He did not receive
a salary but worked tirelessly 24 hours a day to please
his parents. Bear was a rescue dog that turned around
and showered myself, my wife Sherri, his grandparents
Jean, Bob and Nancy and every person and animal he met
(maybe not rabbits) with friendship and love. He made a
lot of people smile every day.

We wanted you to know that a portion of the profits of this
book will be donated to The Humane Society of
the United States.

–Douglas & Sherri Brown

THE HUMANE SOCIETY
OF THE UNITED STATES ©

The human-animal bond is as old as human history. We cherish our animal companions for their unconditional affection and acceptance. We feel a thrill when we glimpse wild creatures in their natural habitat or in our own backyard.

Unfortunately, the human-animal bond has at times been weakened. Humans have exploited some animal species to the point of extinction.

The Humane Society of the United States makes a difference in the lives of animals here at home and worldwide. The HSUS is dedicated to creating a world where our relationship with animals is guided by compassion. We seek a truly humane society in which animals are respected for their intrinsic value, and where the human-animal bond is strong.

Want to help animals? We have plenty of suggestions. Adopt a pet from a local shelter, join The Humane Society and be a part of our work to help companion animals and wildlife. You will be funding our educational, legislative, investigative and outreach projects in the U.S. and across the globe.

Or perhaps you'd like to make a memorial donation in honor of a pet, friend or relative? You can through our Kindred Spirits program. And if you'd like to contribute in a more structured way, our Planned Giving Office has suggestions about estate planning, annuities, and even gifts of stock that avoid capital gains taxes.

Maybe you have land that you would like to preserve as a lasting habitat for wildlife. Our Wildlife Land Trust can help you. Perhaps the land you want to share is a backyard—that's enough. Our Urban Wildlife Sanctuary Program will show you how to create a habitat for your wild neighbors.

So you see, it's easy to help animals. And The HSUS is here to help.

The Humane Society of the United States
2100 L Street NW
Washington, DC 20037
202-452-1100
www.hsus.org

★ TABLE OF CONTENTS ★

Foreword 11

Introduction 15

PART 1: HOW TO BECOME A U.S. CITIZEN

Chapter 1:
Before You Begin Your Journey

What is the USCIS 21

What is a Citizen.. 24

U.S. Citizen 33

Naturalized Citizen 33

Permanent Resident.. 33

Refugees and Persons Seeking Asylum.................................... 34

Nonimmigrants... 34

Parolees.. 34

Undocumented Immigrants..34

Dual Citizenship 34

Chapter 2:
What Does Citizenship Involve?

The Application...38

The Citizenship Test 41

Chapter 3:
Are You Eligible to Become a U.S. Citizen?

Age 45

Legal Status...46

Good Moral Character...47

Loyalty to the U.S. 49

Residence and Physical Presence 50

Military...51

Rights You have 52

Responsibilities You Have 53

Chapter 4:
Eligibility Requirements for Naturalization

The Green Card (Visa)...55

Application Process...56

Green Card Eligibility...58

Chapter 5:
Methods for Obtaining a Green Card

Obtaining a Visa through Family Connections 64

Obtaining a Visa through Marriage to a
U.S. Citizen 66

Obtaining a Visa through Employment 68

Obtaining a Visa through the Diversity
Lottery Program 71

Obtaining a Visa through Investment 74

Obtaining a Visa through Humanitarian Benefits 77

Resources for Further Information 86

Chapter 6:
Form N-400

Cover Letter 90

Application for Naturalization 91

Biometrics 95

Your Green Card 96

Fees 96

One Last Note 97

Chapter 7:
The Interview

Personal Questions 99

English Comprehension 101

Interview Tips 102

After the Interview 105

In Conclusion 106

Part 2: How to Study to Become a U.S. Citizen

Chapter 8:
Learning About American History & Government

Early America 109

The U.S. Constitution 112

Three Branches of the U.S. Government 116

The President... 117

Political Parties in the U.S............................. 119

Notable U.S. Presidents............................... 120

U.S. Presidents Since 1980 124

The Court System 128

Major U.S. Historical Events 129

Chapter 9:
English Skills

Practice Exercises for the English
Language Requirement 137

Genres.. 140

Vocabulary Exercise 141

Chapter 10:
The U.S. Constitution

Principles of the U.S. Constitution 143

The Legislative Branch................................. 144

The Executive Branch................................. 145

The Judicial Branch 146

The Bill of Rights 147

Chapter 11:
The New Citizenship Exam

Which Test to Take 151

Practice Test 152

Chapter 12:
Case Studies

Words From the People 175

Words from the Lawyers 183

Appendix A:
Countries Approving Dual Citizenship

.... 193

Appendix B:
USCIS Service Centers

.... 195

Appendix C:
Immigration Acts

.... 197

Appendix D: New Information and Proposed Legislation 199

Appendix E: USCIS Fee Schedule 201

Appendix F: Presidents 207

Appendix G: The Constitution 211

Appendix H: The Amendments 229

Appendix I: Test Answers 243

Bibliography 255

Author Biography 257

Glossary 259

Index 283

★ FOREWORD ★

By Andrea R. Jacobs, Esq.

America is indeed the land of opportunity! Thus, many foreign-born nationals endeavor to immigrate here and to eventually become U.S. citizens. However, the immigration process can be long and arduous for some people. *Your U.S. Citizen Guide* is a user-friendly handbook which can greatly simplify the naturalization process.

I have been an immigration attorney for almost 20 years, and I can honestly say that this book will help anyone with a simple naturalization case. Of course, anyone who does not understand the forms or the process should consult with an immigration attorney for specific legal advice regarding their case and this is especially true if the person was ever convicted of any crime. Applying for naturalization with a criminal record could lead to a removal process which may very well strip the individual of their residency.

The basis for our naturalization process is "good moral character." If an applicant can demonstrate this trait over the five year period preceding their application, then chances are that they will become a U.S. citizen. In order to prove good moral character, Immigration looks at such characteristics as criminal records, timely child support payment history, and payment of federal and state income taxes.

Another important factor in determining eligibility for citizenship is physical presence. An applicant must be present for more than half of the prescribed residency period. For a naturalization applicant who must be a resident for five years before applying, this prescribed period is more than thirty months. The actual days must be calculated, and the applicant cannot be out of the country for more than six months at any one time, except in limited circumstances. Many applications are denied each year due to improper calculations.

Your U.S. Citizen Guide gives the one hundred most often used examination questions. The officer at the interview will ask the applicant to orally answer six or seven of these questions. If the applicant answers these questions correctly, the officer will move onto the written portion by asking the applicant to write one sentence in English. Many of my clients have anxiety about the examination, but in the past 18 years, I have not had any client fail this component.

In conclusion, use this handbook as a tool to help you prepare for your naturalization process. You should always check with the USCIS to ensure you have the latest version of the form and the correct mailing address. If you have any issues or questions, check with an immigration lawyer. Welcome to the land of opportunity!

Andrea R. Jacobs, P.A.
Immigration & Bankruptcy Law

Andrea R. Jacobs, Esq.
Immigration Attorney
Andrea R. Jacobs, P.A.
11555 Heron Bay Blvd.
Suite 102
Coral Springs, FL 33076
(800)424-7745
andrea@arjlaw.com
www.arjlaw.com

Andrea R. Jacobs, Esquire is the founding attorney of Andrea R. Jacobs, P.A. located in Coral Springs, Florida. Her practice focuses on immigration law and bankruptcy law. Jacobs is a member of the Florida Bar. She is also a member of The United States District Court for The Southern District of Florida.

Prior to starting her own firm in 1993, Jacobs was associated with The Law Offices of Ellen M. Law, P.A.,

Atlas, Pearlman & Trop, P.A. and Smith & Berman, P.A. also located in South Florida. During 1988 and 1989, Jacobs worked in the legal department of the Dole Fresh Fruit Company.

Originally from Rockland County, New York, Jacobs attended high school in Coral Springs, Florida. Jacobs received her Bachelor of Arts, cum laude, from The Honors College at the University of Miami where she majored in English with a minor in Business Administration. Jacobs then attended the University of Florida, College of Law in Gainesville, Florida where her studies included curriculum in the fields of corporate, estate, family law, and tax law. Jacobs received her degree of Doctor of Jurisprudence in 1990.

Jacobs is a member of The American Immigration Lawyers Association, The Florida Bar Association, The Broward Resource League, The American Bar Association, The Florida Association of Women Lawyers, The University of Florida Alumni Association, and Phi Kappa Phi Honorary.

★ INTRODUCTION ★

Congratulations! You want to join the legions of individuals who are American citizens.

With this book, you will learn much, and save time and money. The information in this book will be helpful and will serve as a map to lead you through the naturalization process. Be sure to read it carefully, and pay attention to detail. There are some drawbacks to the do-it-yourself method, but the majority of applicants will have no difficulty at all. Their application will be submitted, it will be processed in a timely manner, and the outcome will be a happy and positive one.

Some applicants' circumstances are not so simple. If you have a complicated situation, you might want to consider consulting an attorney or a paralegal. If you do decide to seek legal assistance, it is important to find an attorney who is an authority on the laws regarding immigration and citizenship. Your local bar association will be happy to provide you with referrals, or you can gather recommendations from friends and relatives.

This book will take you through the steps of becoming

a U.S. citizen. Citizenship is the legal status bestowed on members of the United States by the United States Citizenship and Immigration Services (USCIS). Naturalized citizens have the same rights, duties, and privileges as those who achieve citizenship by birth.

The process of applying for naturalization is often complicated. Just understanding the eligibility requirements and finding the correct category can be daunting and is not for the faint of heart. This book will serve as a blueprint and will help those applying for U.S. citizenship to do so in an organized and sequential manner.

Do not become distressed because the application process can be long and complicated. This book is here to guide you step-by-step through the process and serve as an aid and reference manual. While the information contained in this book is factual and will help you through the naturalization process, you may find it best and easiest to speak to an attorney, especially for complicated circumstances.

Please keep in mind that there are many Internet resources out there to help you acquire U.S. citizenship; however, there are some that charge you for their services. Never pay money to any Web site to have them fill out applications for you. Remember, U.S. government Web sites end in the extension .gov. If the Web site that you are using does not end in .gov then you may be receiving inaccurate information or someone may be trying to take your money.

This new book will inform you about the eligibility rules, provide instructions concerning the application forms, and help you prepare for the interview and the citizenship tests. You will read a study guide on the principles of the U.S. Constitution. You will improve your English and become knowledgeable about the United States and about the benefits and responsibilities of being a citizen. After receiving application instructions, sample test questions, and information about the interview, you will find yourself taking the Oath of Citizenship in record time.

This book is divided into three parts. Part 1 will guide you through what you will need to become a U.S. citizen and explain the processes that you will be going through. Part 2 gives you study materials so that you can prepare yourself for passing the interview and citizenship tests. The accompanying CD-ROM will also provide you with the forms that you will need to fill out and other useful materials.

Again, congratulations on your quest to U.S. citizenship. You will be bleeding red, white, and blue in no time.

★ AMERICAN FACT: *THE WHITE HOUSE* ★

The White House is the official residence and principal workplace of the President of the United States. Located at 1600 Pennsylvania Avenue NW in Washington, D.C., it was built between 1792 and 1800 of white-painted Aquia sandstone in the late Georgian style and has been the executive residence of every U.S. President since John Adams. Today, the White House Complex includes the Executive Residence (in which the First Family resides), the West Wing (the location of the Oval Office, Cabinet Room, and Roosevelt Room), and the East Wing (the location of the office of the First Lady and White House Social Secretary), as well as the Old Executive Office Building, which houses the executive offices of the President and Vice President.

Source: http://en.wikipedia.org/wiki/White_house

PART 1

HOW TO BECOME
★ A U.S. CITIZEN ★

★ AMERICAN FACT: *THE PENTAGON* ★

The Pentagon is the headquarters of the United States Department of Defense, located in Arlington County, Virginia. As a symbol of the U.S. military, "the Pentagon" is often used metonymically to refer to the Department of Defense rather than the building itself. Designed by the American architect George Bergstrom, the building was dedicated on January 15, 1943. The Pentagon is the world's largest office building. It houses approximately 23,000 military and civilian employees and about 3,000 non-defense support personnel. It has five sides, five floors above ground (plus two basement levels), and five ring corridors per floor with a total of 17.5 miles of corridors. The Pentagon includes a five-acre central plaza, shaped like a pentagon.

Source: http://en.wikipedia.org/wiki/The_Pentagon

1
BEFORE YOU BEGIN
★ YOUR JOURNEY ★

Over 7.5 million applications and petitions are received each year by the United States government. These applications come from people who want to immigrate to the United States, people in the United States that want to become a citizen, people who are trying to gain citizenship for members of their family, and many more.

To process these applications and petitions, the United States created a special division of the government called the United States Citizenship and Immigration Service (USCIS).

WHAT IS THE USCIS?

The United States Citizenship and Immigration Service (USCIS), formerly the Immigration and Naturalization Service (INS), became a division of the United States Department of Homeland Security on March 1, 2003. The department is responsible for the administration of the immigration and naturalization process, including all services, polices, and priorities that relate to immigration and naturalization.

One of the department's many functions is to process visa petitions, petitions for naturalization, and asylum and refugee applications. The USCIS also manages all other functions related to immigration, including the processing of asylum claims, the administration of immigrant benefits and services, and the issuance of employment authorization documents.

The USCIS consists of over 15,000 federal employees and contractors who staff 250 field offices around the globe.

The USCIS contains many different offices, including the Office of Citizenship and the Refugee, Asylum, and International Operations Directorate.

The Office of Citizenship

The Office of Citizenship helps educate immigrates about becoming a U.S. citizen. Not only do they help educate immigrants about the process of becoming a U.S. citizen, they also provide them with the necessary tools and information they need to help integrate them successfully into American culture. The Office of Citizenship provides this knowledge when immigrants first become permanent residents of the U.S. and then again when they begin the naturalization process.

The Refugee, Asylum, and International Operations Directorate

The Refugee, Asylum, and International Operations Directorate (RAIO) oversees, plans, and implements all policies that are related to asylum and refugee issues, and they also help with immigration in foreign countries.

The RAIO contains three distinct divisions: The Refugee Affairs Division, The Asylum Division, and the International Operations Division.

The Refugee Affairs Division

The Refugee Affairs Division partners with the United States Refugee Admission Program to provide humanitarian benefit to refugee resettlement. Refugees are people who flee from a country because of their safety and are unable to return because of persecution or a fear of persecution because of their race, religion, nationality, or membership in a group. This status has to be formally decided by the Refugee Affairs Division before a refugee can be allowed to resettle within the U.S. borders. Refugees are granted legal resident status.

The Asylum Division

The Asylum Division oversees the U.S. affirmative asylum process. This process permits individuals who are already in the U.S. or at a U.S. port of entry who are not already in immigration proceedings to request asylum because they are not able or unwilling to return to their native country because of persecution or a fear of persecution because of their race, religion, nationality, or membership in a group. The main distinction between an asylee and a refugee is that an asylee applies for residency while on U.S. soil; a refugee applies for residency while still in another country.

The International Operations Directorate

The International Operations Directorate operates overseas, and is the face of the USCIS in other countries. This division has 30 international field offices. This division is responsible for extending immigration opportunities and benefits to eligible individuals.

WHAT IS A CITIZEN?

The Statue of Liberty is an American icon and one of the best-known symbols in the world. It represents freedom and refuge from oppression. The statue depicts an upright female figure holding a torch in her right hand.

Beginning in the late 1800s, thousands of immigrants came through Ellis Island in New York to seek "life, liberty, and the pursuit of happiness." The Statue of Liberty was one of the first things the weary travelers saw. Lady Liberty still reigns over New York Harbor, a reminder to all of us that we are a "nation of immigrants" and a "melting pot" of nationalities.

The United States Citizenship and Immigration Services (USCIS) bestow U.S. citizenship on new Americans. When a person from another country becomes a U.S. citizen, he or she is called a "naturalized citizen." Naturalized citizens and those who achieve citizenship by birth have the same rights, freedoms, duties, and responsibilities of citizenship.

Rights and Responsibilities of U.S. Citizens

A U.S. citizen has all rights guaranteed in the U.S.

Constitution, and is subject to all U.S. laws. All U.S. citizens have a right to life, liberty, and property.

The U.S. Constitution was written in 1787 and outlines the basic principles of the U.S. government. This document can be amended as necessary, though amendments are rare. You will learn more about this process in later chapters of this book.

The original states appointed representatives to sign the Constitution and agree on the general principles. The Constitution begins with a preamble, which has the beginning phrase, "We the People." Granted, at this time, "We the People" was only white men.

The preamble lists what American citizens have a duty to do in order to form a more perfect union. These duties are detailed throughout the Constitution:

- Establish justice

- Ensure domestic tranquility

- Provide for the common defense

- Promote the general welfare

- Secure the blessings of liberty

Not all people were satisfied with the Constitution because it did not outline specific rights to citizens. The framers of the Constitution also drafted the Bill of Rights, which contained the first 10 amendments. The Constitution has been amended 27 times, though the 18th amendment was rescinded, so only 26 amendments are in effect.

Amendments give the government a way to protect specific freedoms and expand freedoms. Through amendments, voting rights have been extended to African Americans, women, Native Americans, and citizens that are 18. These amendments are always up for interpretation from the U.S. Supreme Court.

Citizens have a duty to know and learn about the government and take part in the government on issues that concern their lives. Namely, one of the greatest responsibilities and rights of U.S. citizens is the right to vote. Voting gives citizens the power to take part in the government and have a say in any and all laws that might be made. Voting allows citizens to directly voice their opinions on issues and elect representatives that will best represent their voices on other issues that they do not have a direct vote in.

Amendment 14 of the U.S. Constitution states: "All persons born or naturalized in the United States, and subject to the jurisdiction thereof, are citizens of the United States and of the state wherein they reside. No state shall make or enforce any law which shall abridge the privileges or immunities of citizens of the United States; nor shall any state deprive any person of life, liberty, or property, without due process of law; nor deny to any person within its jurisdiction the equal protection of the laws."

Privileges of U.S. Citizens

Once a person takes the Oath of Allegiance, he or she

acquires all the rights and responsibilities of U.S. citizenship. For example, new citizens are allowed to vote and run for political office. California Governor Arnold Schwarzenegger is not a U.S. citizen by birth; however, as a naturalized citizen he is allowed the privilege to vote and run for office. One privilege that is not applicable to naturalized citizens who are not born in the U.S. is the ability to run for U.S. president or vice president.

Duties of U.S. Citizens

Many of the rights and freedoms of citizenship are earned by exercising duties and obligations. To protect democracy, citizens of a free nation must be willing to take part in the process of government. There are many responsibilities that come along with a new citizen's rights and freedoms.

Citizens are expected to be loyal to their country, respect the laws, and contribute to the success of the United States of America. Specific duties include:

- **Jury duty:** You may be asked by the government to serve on a jury. Jury service is an obligation of citizens. As a U.S. citizen, your name will automatically be placed on the list of prospective jurors.

  Many people think that you must be registered to vote to receive a jury summons; however, this is not always true. Local governments pull from a list of names from other sources, including those who have registered for a license and pay taxes.

Every state has different laws regarding jury duty. To find out more, it is best to check with your own state. You cannot serve as a member of the jury if you are not a U.S. citizen and if you do not speak English.

To notify you that you have jury duty, your local government will mail you a summons telling you that you have been requested for jury duty on a specific date. You will need to inform your employer about your summons (this missed work day is excused), and you will need to show up at your summons or you can be fined and held in contempt of the court.

Make sure that you carefully read your summons letter to know how to respond. Some states may make you fill out a questionnaire and send it in before reporting to jury duty.

- **Obeying the laws:** Citizens must be loyal to the United States and abide by federal, state, and local laws.

  However, do not be misled. Anyone living in the U.S. is subject to U.S. laws. One great difference in the laws regarding U.S. citizens versus non-U.S. citizens is what happens if you break the law.

  Illegal citizens may be deported for breaking the law. U.S. citizens, on the other hand, have the legal right to an attorney and a jury of their peers.

- **Taxes:** The 16th amendment requires all persons

residing in the United States to pay federal, state, and local taxes.

Taxes serve four purposes: revenue, redistribution, repricing, and representation.

The amount of taxes you pay will vary by city and state. Federal and state taxes are usually filed by April 15. These taxes are usually withheld from each paycheck that you receive. If you do not hold back enough money, you may be required to pay the government; however, if you hold back too much money, then the government will issue you a check. Filing taxes is different for every individual, so it is best for you to check with an accountant at tax time to ensure that you receive the maximum deductions possible.

Local taxes vary and may need to be paid at different times throughout the year. In Florida, for example, you are required to pay for your vehicle registration. This payment is due on your birthday, and you will receive a notice in the mail about one month prior to your birthday.

Other local taxes may apply, such as property taxes, road assessment taxes, school taxes, and so on. You will need to familiarize yourself with the laws of the area that you plan to live in and plan accordingly.

- **Voting in elections:** Voting is a right, but it should also be viewed as an obligation. The only way citizens can influence the government and have a voice in government decisions is by voting. Citizens should cast their votes in federal, state, and local elections. It is also important for citizens to become knowledgeable about the issues, so they can use their votes in a careful, responsible manner. Every voter should make an effort to judge the merits of the candidates so that only the best contenders get elected to office.

- **Participating in political parties:** Citizens should exercise their right to self-government by participating in political parties.

When you register to vote you will be asked which political party that you want to be affiliated with. You can choose "none," or you can choose something else. Most U.S. citizens are listed as either Democrats or Republicans; however, there are multiple parties that you can affiliate yourself with. It is best to do research on the individual parties and see which one fits your beliefs the best.

- **Defending the country:** Citizens may choose to defend the United States by serving in the armed forces.

By law, all men aged 18 to 26 who live in the U.S. must register with the Selective Service. Just because you register does not mean that you will serve in the armed services. The Selective Service keeps a list of names in case a need for a military draft arises.

Women do not have to register for the Selective Service; however, women can still serve in the armed forces. Women cannot be drafted.

If you wish to serve in the armed forces, you may go to an armed forces recruiter once you are 18 and a U.S. citizen. They will be able to instruct you on how to join whichever branch of the military that you wish to join.

Benefits of U.S. Citizenship

Many benefits and privileges are available to U.S. citizens, including the following:

- Security from the threat of deportation

- Eligibility for some government jobs

- Many public benefits

- Freedom to travel in and out of the country at will

- Ease of bringing in family members

Drawbacks to Applying for U.S. Citizenship

There are many advantages to applying for citizenship, but, for some people, there may also be disadvantages, and it can be an emotionally wrenching decision for some. Before making the decision to apply for naturalization, you should also consider the following possible drawbacks:

- When a person initiates the naturalization process, the USCIS examines the applicant's history. If the person has been convicted of criminal acts, acquired his or her green card illegally, or has become deportable since receiving permanent residence status, his or her application for naturalization will be denied. Applicants who have concerns about the above possibilities should consult an authority on immigration law before applying for U.S. citizenship.

- Not all countries permit dual citizenship. Even when an applicant's native country does allow dual citizenship, some benefits may be forfeited if he or she becomes a U.S. citizen.

- Applicants who journey into countries that are unfriendly to the U.S. may be at risk if they have an American passport.

- When an individual becomes an American citizen, he or she must relinquish allegiance to other nations. This means that an applicant may not be able to defend his or her home country in a time of war.

It is very important to weigh the benefits against the possible risks and disadvantages before applying for U.S. citizenship.

This rest of this chapter gives a brief overview of the legal status of immigrants and citizens. The ensuing chapters will go into greater depth on the classifications of legal status.

U.S. CITIZEN

A U.S. citizen is a person who was born in the United States or was born in another country to parents who are U.S. citizens, who are naturalized citizens, or foreign children under the age of 18 who are adopted by U.S. citizens and immigrate to the U.S.

NATURALIZED CITIZEN

After an individual immigrates, acquires a green card, and waits out the required time, he or she is eligible to apply for U.S. citizenship. After the process of naturalization has been completed, the applicant's legal status is that of citizen of the United States. No one is more of a citizen or less of a citizen. Naturalized citizens and those who achieve citizenship by birth have the same rights, duties, and privileges, and you will have the right to just and equal treatment under the laws of the United States.

PERMANENT RESIDENT

Permanent residents are people who hold green cards. A lawful permanent resident has the right to reside and work in the United States. In most cases, a person has to be a permanent resident for five years before applying to become a naturalized citizen of the United States. However, if an individual is married to and living with a spouse who is a U.S. citizen and has been a citizen for at least three years prior to application, the waiting period is only three years.

REFUGEES AND PERSONS SEEKING ASYLUM

People who have a real and valid fear of persecution in their home country due to race, religion, or political perspective are considered refugees or persons seeking asylum.

NONIMMIGRANTS

Nonimmigrants are those who come to the United States temporarily for a specific purpose and for a limited period. Some people, such as students, tourists, persons engaged in commerce, and temporary workers, enter the United States on a nonimmigrant visa.

PAROLEES

A parolee is an individual who is allowed temporary entrance due to an emergency family situation or for humanitarian reasons.

UNDOCUMENTED IMMIGRANTS

A person is an undocumented immigrant if he or she resides within the borders of the United States, but has no legal right to be here.

DUAL CITIZENSHIP

An individual has dual citizenship if he or she is a citizen of two countries at the same time. This means that the person must obey the laws of both countries and pay taxes for both countries. Dual citizenship sometimes occurs automatically. If a person is born abroad to American parents, he or she is automatically a citizen of both countries. If an individual is born in the U.S. to parents who are citizens of another country, he or she is automatically a citizen of both countries.

Every country has its own laws concerning citizenship. Upon becoming a naturalized citizen, the U.S. requires a person to relinquish his or her allegiance to any other country. Some countries refuse to acknowledge this renunciation and will regard a naturalized U.S. citizen as a citizen of both nations. Others do not allow dual citizenship, which means that if you become a naturalized U.S. citizen, you will be required to give up your other citizenship. It is important for an applicant for U.S. citizenship to consider this issue carefully.

When an individual forfeits allegiance to another country, he or she is not necessarily relinquishing citizenship in that country. It means that if the two countries become involved in war, the person will defend the U.S. rather than his or her native land. (See Appendix A for a list of countries that allow dual citizenship). The question of dual citizenship can be important. By giving up citizenship in his or her native country, a person may also be giving up some of the rights and benefits enjoyed as a citizen of that country. Applicants who have concerns about this issue should consult the embassy of their home country to find out about the laws concerning dual citizenship.

★ AMERICAN FACT: *THE STATUE OF LIBERTY* ★

The Statue of Liberty was presented to the United States by the people of France in 1886. Standing on Liberty Island in New York Harbor, it welcomes visitors, immigrants, and returning Americans traveling by ship. The statue itself is 151 feet tall, but with the pedestal and foundation, it stands 305 feet tall.

Source: http://en.wikipedia.org/wiki/Statue_of_liberty

2
WHAT DOES
★ CITIZENSHIP INVOLVE? ★

The United States is a nation of immigrants. When a person immigrates to the U.S. and applies for naturalization, he or she joins a long line of people who have done so. This chapter gives a brief overview of the process of naturalization. The ensuing chapters will provide more detailed information on each step of the procedure, so that you will be able to make an informed decision about becoming a naturalized citizen.

Keep in mind that as an applicant for naturalization, you must be admitted to the U.S. as a lawful permanent resident (possess a green card). You should also have at least five years of continuous residence. Continuous residence does not mean that you have physically lived in the U.S. for the entire five years, but you will have to have proof, such as a mailing address, or documentation saying you have paid U.S. taxes, to confirm this residency requirement. If you are traveling overseas for more than a few months, it is advisable to get a travel document before departing. This can be done by filling out Form I-131. You will, however, need to have actual physical residence in the state you are applying for three months prior to filing for naturalization.

There is an exception to the rule for being a lawful resident for people who have served in the U.S. armed forces during war. These people can become a naturalized citizen without first becoming a permanent resident.

To become a U.S. citizen, you will also need to have and demonstrate the ability to read, write, and speak English, unless physically unable to do so, such as the case with being blind or deaf. You will also need to have a good moral character and show your allegiance to the U.S. Constitution. You will need to show your understanding of U.S. history and the U.S. government. To file, you will also need to be at least 18 years old, although there are exceptions for children of permanent residents who are seeking naturalization.

THE APPLICATION

The first step in applying for U.S. citizenship is to file a "petition for naturalization." Do not pay for the application materials. The forms can be obtained free from the USCIS. You may go online to their Web site and download the forms at **www.uscis.gov**, or you can obtain a copy from the accompanying CD-ROM. There are two PDFs. One contains the instructions, which you need to read thoroughly, and the other contains the actual N-400 form, which you will need to complete.

The packet will include an Application for Naturalization

(N-400), a biographical information sheet, and a fingerprint chart. Three unsigned photographs of the applicant's face should be included with the completed package.

The USCIS materials will include detailed instructions for completing the forms. Below is a list of the basic steps:

- Complete the application fully and accurately.

- Fill out the biographical information form. The information requested will be similar to the questions asked on the application form.

- Record personal information, such as name, address, and date of birth on the biometric chart. The USCIS will instruct you when and where to get your biometric scan.

- Be sure to fill out the forms carefully and tell the exact truth. Under the Immigration and Nationality Act, a person must tell the truth and give the correct information to the USCIS. An entire history must be included, even if it involves criminal convictions. The examiner will expect a response to the same questions during the interview. If any statements are untruthful, citizenship may be denied.

It costs money to apply for U.S. citizenship. The fee for the N-400 packet is $595 plus a biometrics fee of $80, bringing the total charge to $675. If you are over 75 years old, then you do not need to include the biometric fee, making your total only $595. There is no fee for military applicants who are filing under Section 328 and 329 of the INA.

You can find a full listing of fees associated with different forms and applications dealing with immigration and naturalization in Appendix E.

Send your N-400 application, supporting documents, and payment to the service center having jurisdiction over your place of residence.

The service centers are as follows:

If you live in AZ, CA, HI, NV, Territory of Guam, or the Commonwealth of the Northern Mariana Islands, send your N-400 application to:

California Service Center
P.O. Box 10400
Laguna Niguel, CA 92607-1040

If you live in AK, CO, ID, IL, IN, IA, KS, MI, MO, MN, MT, NE, ND, OH, OR, SD, UT, WA, WI, or WY, send your N-400 application to:

Nebraska Service Center
P.O. Box 87400
Lincoln, NE 68501-7400

If you live in AL, AR, FL, GA, KY, LA, MS, NM, NC, OK, SC, TN, or TX, send your N-400 application to:

Texas Service Center
P.O. Box 851204
Mesquite, TX 75185-1204

If you live in CT, DE, District of Columbia, ME, MD, MA, NH, NJ, NY, PA, RI, VT, VA, WV, Commonwealth of Puerto Rico, or the U.S. Virgin Islands, send your N-400 application to:

Vermont Service Center
75 Lower Welden St.
St. Albans, VT 05479-9400

If you are filing for naturalization under military provisions, section 328 or 329, then you should send your application to the Nebraska Service Center no matter your geographical location. Send your application to:

Nebraska Service Center
P.O. Box 87426
Lincoln, NE 68501-7426

THE CITIZENSHIP TEST

The U.S. History and Government Test

An applicant for citizenship must be able to show knowledge and understanding of basic American history and government.

The test will contain 7-10 questions from a set of 100 multiple choice questions, which will ask you about the U.S. Constitution and amendments, U.S. history from the forming of the U.S. to the current day, past and present U.S. presidents, and much more. You only need to get 70 percent of these questions correct in order to pass.

To help prepare you for this test, you can find out

information about U.S. history and current-day policies in Chapter 13. You can find out more information about the Constitution in Chapters 13 and 15. Chapter 16 presents what you need to know about the test and also contains a sample 100-question test that you can take and use to help study.

If you fail the test, you will have a second opportunity to retake it based on the same application. If you fail the second time, you will have to submit a new application.

The Interview

After you file your petition, you will be scheduled for an interview with USCIS. Do not lose your interview notice; you will need it to get inside the USCIS building. When you enter the building, you will be processed through security. The location of your interview will likely be in the district where you live. If you move, be sure to notify the USCIS of your new location. You will need to submit an AR-11 form and a change of address notice to the local office.

Witnesses are no longer required, but you can bring a witness if you need someone to verify that you are eligible to become a naturalized citizen. During the interview, you will be required to show that you can read, write, and speak English. The USCIS examiner will also review your application to make certain that all your statements are true. You will be asked to show your tax returns or explain why you were not required to file a tax return. In addition, you should bring the following original documents to the interview with you:

- Driver's license, state-issued ID, or passport

- Work permit

- Original birth certificate

- Original marriage certificate

- Approval notices

An applicant for U.S. citizenship must have an interview. The purpose of the interview is twofold. One is to show that you are competent in the English language, and it is also to give your allegiance to the United States.

At the interview, you will need to show your ability to read, write, speak, and understand basic words in the English language. This will be done through a means of reading and speaking. You will be asked questions about your N-400 application as well as government questions.

Some people are exempt from the knowledge requirement if the following applies on the date of application:

- The person seeking naturalization is a legal resident, is over 50 years of age, and has been living in the U.S. for over 20 years.

- The applicant is a legal resident, is over 55 years of age, and has been living in the United States for at least 15 years.

- The applicant can establish a physical or mental condition that affects his or her ability to learn English.

If you fail the English competence part of the interview, you will have a second opportunity to retake it based on the same application. If you fail the second time, you will have to submit a new application.

You can read more about the interview process and prepare for the English test in Chapter 14.

You will also need to show your allegiance to the United States. You will need to state that you agree with the principles of the U.S. Constitution.

After the interview is over and the petition for naturalization has been filed, a final court appearance will be scheduled. At this hearing, the examiner will verify that all requirements for naturalization have been met, and the applicant will be asked to repeat the Oath of Allegiance and vow to defend the U.S. Constitution and support the laws of the United States.

The Swearing-In Ceremony

After your interview, you will receive a notice in the mail about your ceremony date from the USCIS.

You will go to this ceremony, along with other people who are becoming naturalized U.S. citizens. Here, you will check in, return your permanent resident card, answer questions about what you have done since your interview, take the naturalization oath, and receive your certificate of naturalization.

3
ARE YOU ELIGIBLE TO
★ BECOME A U.S. CITIZEN? ★

To become a U.S. citizen, an applicant must meet certain requirements as follows: He or she must be able to read, write, and understand English and have a basic knowledge of American history, the U.S. government, and the Constitution. In addition, the applicant must:

- Be at least 18 years of age

- Have been a legal resident for at least five years

- Be of good moral character

- Be loyal to the U.S., and be willing to take an oath of allegiance

AGE

You need to be at least 18 years old to apply for U.S. citizenship. If you are under 18, you need to find out about the legal position of your mother and father in regard to citizenship. It is possible that you are a U.S. citizen by virtue of your parents' status. If you were born in the United States or in a territory of the United States, you became a U.S. citizen at birth.

Derivative Beneficiaries

A derivative beneficiary is the child or spouse of the person on whose behalf the petition is filed. There are no derivative beneficiaries in immediate-relative family-based cases, which means that each applicant must have his or her own petition and individual case number. Form I-360 may be completed by a non-U.S. citizen when applying for certain benefits granted to special immigrants including, but not limited to: widow(er)s, Amerasians, children of U.S. citizens, and battered spouses. Individuals who do not provide truthful information may experience criminal or civil prosecution. Further consequences include denial of the application, fines, and/or imprisonment. The individual may also lose future immigration benefits. Form I-360 (Petition for Amerasian, Widow(er), or Special Immigrant) may also be known as USCIS Form I-360, I 360, Form I360 or immigration form I-360.

LEGAL STATUS

To obtain legal status, you must have been legally admitted into the U.S. for permanent residence. This means that you need to have an Alien Registration Receipt Card (a green card) and be able to produce it to show your legal status.

Spouses of U.S. Citizens

If you are a legal, permanent resident married to a U.S. citizen, you may be considered a "special case." You may be able to file an application for citizenship after only living in the U.S. continuously for three years. The following rules apply:

- You have been lawfully married to the U.S. citizen for at least three years.

- Your spouse has been a citizen for at least three years and has met all the requirements for residency.

- You have met all the other requirements for U.S. citizenship.

Realize that if you do apply for U.S. citizenship by way of marriage, you will need to prove that you are married, and it must not look like you only married to obtain U.S. citizenship. Your case will be taken more seriously if you are able to provide documentation of your relationship, as well as any bills that you and your spouse have that are in both your names.

GOOD MORAL CHARACTER

An applicant must demonstrate that he or she is of good moral character. Morals and values are somewhat objective and, in general, good moral character depends on the values and expectations of the community in which the person lives. However, some issues can affect a determination of whether or not you have good moral character. For example, involvement in the following activities may cause a positive determination:

- Helping out in schools

- Community service

- Religious activities

- Volunteer work

A person who has been involved in certain types of acts is thought to not be of good moral character. The following circumstances may cause a negative determination:

- Failure to pay taxes

- Being addicted to drugs

- Being a polygamist

- Not paying child support

- Neglecting to register with Selective Service (if applicant is a male)

- Drunk driving

- Drinking habitually

- Earning a living as a gambler

- Being untruthful to the USCIS

A conviction for any of the following crimes will weigh heavily against an applicant, may cause his or her application to be denied, and could permanently bar the person from becoming a naturalized U.S. citizen:

- Homicide

- An aggravated felony

- Sale of a controlled substance

- Conviction for possession of a controlled substance (except for 30 grams or less of marijuana)

- Providing false testimony in a court of law

- Earning a living by illegal gambling

- Prostitution

- Involvement in vice and/or organized crime

- Smuggling undocumented aliens into the U.S.

- Conviction of two or more crimes that sent applicant to jail for five years or more

- Confinement to a penal institution during the legal period for a total of 180 days or more

LOYALTY TO THE U.S.

Your actions and behavior while you hold a green card can affect your status if you decide to apply for naturalization. As a permanent resident, you have the privilege of living and working in the United States. To prove that you are loyal to the United States, you should not live in another country or support another country in time of war. This is not to say that you cannot still cheer for your old country's soccer team at the Olympics.

If your application for citizenship is accepted, you will take the citizenship oath and swear allegiance to the United States. You will show your loyalty to the U.S. by the following:

- Your willingness to defend the U.S. Constitution

- Obeying the laws of the United States

- Giving up any prior allegiances to other countries

- Serving the United States during times of war or national emergency

RESIDENCE AND PHYSICAL PRESENCE

An applicant is eligible to file for citizenship if, immediately preceding the filing of the application, he or she:

- Is a lawful permanent resident.

- Has lived in the U.S. as a lawful, permanent resident for a period of five or more years before application.

- Has maintained a physical presence in the United States for 30 months or more during the previous five-year period. If the applicant has lived outside the United States for more than six months, but less than 12 months, continuity of residence is interrupted (unless the applicant can prove that he or she did not abandon his place of residence during the legal period).

- Has lived in a particular state for at least 90 days.

MILITARY

Veterans of U.S. Armed Forces

Special consideration is sometimes given to persons who performed honorable service to the U.S. during a time of war. If an applicant served during any of the time periods below, he or she can file the N-400 Military Naturalization Packet to request special consideration for military service:

- **World War I** – April 16, 1916 to November 11, 1918

- **World War II** – September 1, 1939 to December 31, 1946

- **Korean Conflict** – June 25, 1950 to July 1, 1955

- **Vietnam War** – February 28, 1961 to October 15, 1978

- **Operation Desert Shield/Desert Storm** – August 29, 1990 to April 11, 1991

Other Exemptions for Military Service

If you are a legal permanent resident, have served for three years or longer in the U.S. military, and file your application for naturalization while you are still actively serving or within six months of an honorable discharge, you may be exempted from the requirement for a specific period of residence.

There is sometimes an exception if you are a lawful,

permanent resident married to a U.S. citizen stationed outside the United States. You may not have to comply with the residency or physical presence requirements if the U.S.-citizen spouse is employed by one of the following:

- The U.S. armed forces or the U.S. government

- A recognized American research institution

- A recognized U.S. religious organization

- An American firm engaged in the development of U.S. commerce in another country

RIGHTS YOU HAVE

Before you become a U.S. citizen, you still have many rights as a lawful permanent resident:

- Purchase or own a firearm, as long as there are no state or local restrictions preventing it

- Request a visa for your husband or wife and unmarried children to live in the U.S.

- Get Social Security, Supplemental Security Income, and Medicare benefits, if you are eligible

- Own property in the U.S.

- Apply for a driver's license in your state or territory

- Leave and return to the U.S. under certain

conditions

RESPONSIBILITIES YOU HAVE

With any rights come responsibilities. Becoming a U.S. citizen bears no exceptions. As a lawful U.S. resident, you will have the following responsibilities:

- You must pay federal, state, and local income taxes.

- You must obey all federal, state, and local laws.

- If you are a male between the ages of 18 and 26, you must register with Selective Service.

- You are required to have your green card available at all times, and show it to an immigration officer if asked to do so.

- You must renew your card before the expiration date.

- You must maintain your immigration status.

- You must not leave the United States for an extended period or move to another country to live there permanently.

You can also find these guidelines on the USCIS Web site, available at **http://www.uscis.gov/portal/site/uscis**.

★ AMERICAN FACT: *THE UNITED STATES CAPITOL* ★

The United States Capitol serves as the seat of government for the United States Congress, the legislative branch of the U.S. federal government. It is located in Washington, D.C., on top of Capitol Hill at the eastern end of the National Mall. The Capitol Grounds cover approximately 274 acres.

Source: http://en.wikipedia.org/wiki/United_States_Capitol

4
ELIGIBILITY REQUIREMENTS
★ FOR NATURALIZATION ★

THE GREEN CARD (VISA)

The green card is the first step to becoming a U.S. citizen. Before an individual can apply for U.S. citizenship, he or she must have a green card (also called a "visa"). The green card establishes a person as a lawful, permanent resident of the United States. This card gives you the ability to live and work in the United States. When applying for jobs in the United States, employers will often ask for you to present your green card for identification purposes. After five years of residence in the United States with the green card, you can then begin the naturalization process.

Do not be misled, though. The green card is not actually green. It gets its name from the days after World War II when the card was printed on green paper. Since 1977, the card has been printed on various papers, none of which were green. Today's card is printed on a yellowish-white paper. The card contains your name and photograph, as well as other information, such as your birthday and signature.

This chapter gives an overview of the ways an individual can obtain a green card. The ensuing chapters will provide more detail on each topic.

APPLICATION PROCESS

The number of green cards given each year varies for each method of application. It can also take several years to process a green card request.

There are generally three steps to applying for a green card. Those are:

1. Immigrant petition

2. Immigrant visa availability

3. Immigrant visa adjudication

Immigrant Petition

An immigrant petition is the first step to obtaining your green card. This step is where the USCIS approves your petition through a qualifying means. There are two ways to qualify: family and employer.

To apply for family-based immigration, you must be a close family member of a U.S. citizen or permanent resident who falls into one of three categories: immediate relatives, close family members, and family members of permanent residents.

There are 140,000 employment-based immigrant visas issued yearly. These visas are divided among five preference categories: priority workers, national-interest waiver, skilled workers (professionals holding degrees), religious workers, and foreign investors.

Immigrant Visa Availability

This is the second step of the green card process, unless you are an immediate relative of a U.S. citizen. An immigrant visa number through the National Visa Center must be available. This number may not be available even if the USCIS approves your petition in the first step, and it may take several years for it to become available. The waiting lists are long because the number of visas is limited each year by quotas set in the Immigration and Nationality Act, and the visa may also be restricted by your country of birth.

Immigrant Visa Adjudication

This is the third and final step in obtaining a U.S. green card. Here, you must apply with the USCIS to adjust your current status to permanent resident status, or you can apply with the Department of State for an immigrant visa at the nearest U.S. consulate. You will need this status changed to be allowed to come to the United States.

There are two ways to complete this step:

1. Adjustment of status (AOS)

2. Consular processing

AOS

Adjustment of status is filed with Form I-485, Application to Register Permanent Residence or Adjust Status, to the USCIS. After getting the application, the USCIS conducts extensive background checks, which include fingerprinting and name checking, to make a decision on your application. After the USCIS accepts the application, then you are allowed to stay in the United States even if the original period of time that is indicated on Form I-94 has expired. However, you are not allowed to leave the country until the application is either rejected or approved. If for some reason you have to leave the country during this time, you can file for travel documents through the USCIS (Form I-131, Advance Parole).

Consular Processing

While an alternative to AOS, this method still requires that the immigrant visa petition be completed. This method is best if you are outside the U.S. You can make an appointment at a U.S. consulate in your country and have a consular offer to examine your case. If approved, you will be issued an immigrant visa stamp in your passport. A few weeks after entrance into the United States, your official green card will be mailed to your U.S. address.

GREEN CARD ELIGIBILITY

Not everyone is eligible for a green card. A green card can be obtained through:

- Family connections

- Marriage to a U.S. citizen

- Employment

- The green card lottery

- Investment

- The humanitarian benefits program

Family Connections

U.S. citizens can sponsor a spouse, parents, brothers and sisters, and married or unmarried sons and daughters. The parent, spouse, or minor child of a U.S. citizen is an immediate relative. These people do not have to wait for a visa number. Processing usually begins upon receipt. There are no restrictions on the number of immediate relatives who can immigrate to the U.S. each year.

There are several requirements. The sponsor must be:

- A citizen or a legal permanent resident

- Able to prove that he or she is a U.S. citizen or a lawful permanent resident

- Willing and able to accept both legal and financial responsibility

- If you are gaining approval through a sibling, then you must have the same parents

- You must be 21 years old to sponsor your parents for a green card

If you are a U.S. citizen parent who is applying for minor children, the following conditions apply:

- The child or children must be under the age of 21 (If the child is 21 or older, he or she falls into a preference category, as discussed later in the chapter).

- A separate I-130 petition must be filed for each child.

- Any children of unmarried minor children may be included.

- A stepparent may apply for a stepchild if the parents' marriage took place before the stepchild turned 18.

- A parent may apply for adopted children if the adoption took place before the child turned 16 and the parent and child have lived together for at least two years.

If you are a U.S. citizen applying for one or both of your parents, the following instructions apply:

- The U.S. citizen child applying for his or her parents must be 21 years of age.

- A separate I-130 petition must be filed for each parent.

- A petition to sponsor parents does not include the minor children of the parents (siblings of the petitioner). These people fall under preference categories. See information on preference categories later on in this chapter.

- The U.S. citizen may apply for a stepparent if the marriage took place before the U.S. citizen child's 18th birthday.

U.S. Citizen Spouses

If you are obtaining a green card via marriage to an American citizen, you may have an advantage. Spouses of U.S. citizens are considered immediate relatives and are not required to wait for a visa number. You must provide documentation to prove a bona fide marriage.

Employment-Based Petitions

You may be able to obtain a visa through employment if a U.S. company offers you a job that you are competent to do. The U.S. employer will have to advertise the job's availability and demonstrate that no qualified U.S. citizens or permanent residents have applied for it.

Investment

To qualify for citizenship by investment, you need to be able to invest between $500,000 and $1 million in capital to form a business where you can employ at least ten U.S. workers. This would qualify you to be able to enter the U.S. with your spouse and children.

The Green Card Lottery

If a person is in a low-preference category, he or she might get a visa faster by entering the Diversity Visa Lottery Program. Every year about 50,000 immigrant visas are distributed to people from countries with low immigration rates. This lottery is based on your birth country, which may not be the same country where you maintain citizenship.

Humanitarian Benefits

In addition to the above categories, immigration law provides several humanitarian-motivated mechanisms to assist individuals who are in need of shelter or aid from various disasters and oppression, such as the following:

- Asylum

- Temporary protected status (TPS)

- Refugee status

- Violence Against Women Act (VAWA)

- Humanitarian parole

5
METHODS FOR OBTAINING
★ A GREEN CARD ★

According to the U.S. Citizenship and Immigration Services (USCIS) Web site (**www.USCIS.gov**), a "green card" gives you official immigration status (Lawful Permanent Residency) in the United States. In the previous chapter, you were briefly introduced to the six ways you can qualify for a visa. You may be eligible for a visa by one of the following means:

- Family connections

- Marriage to a U.S. Citizen

- Employment

- The green card lottery

- Investment

- The humanitarian benefits program

The following sections will provide a more in depth overview of these six ways to obtain a visa in the United State.

OBTAINING A VISA THROUGH FAMILY CONNECTIONS

One of the easiest ways to obtain a U.S. visa is through family connections. This is because the U.S. immigration department wants to reunite families. This method of obtaining a visa allows an eligible family member to apply for a visa on your behalf.

Who is Eligible?

In order for the family member to sponsor your immigration into the United States, the family member must meet the following criteria:

- They must be a citizen or lawful permanent resident of the U.S. and be able to provide documentation providing that status.

- They must prove that they can support you at 125% above the mandated poverty line, by filling out an Affidavit of Support.

The relatives that can be sponsored as an immigrant vary depending on whether the sponsor is a U.S. Citizen or a lawful permanent resident. In any case, the sponsor must be able to provide proof of the relationship

If the sponsor is a U.S. Citizen, they may petition for the following foreign national relatives to immigrate to the U.S.:

- Husband or wife

- Unmarried child under 21 years of age

- Unmarried son or daughter over 21

- Married son or daughter of any age

- Brother or sister, if the sponsor is at least 21 years old

- Parent, if the sponsor is at least 21 years old

If the sponsor is a lawful permanent resident, they may petition for the following foreign national relatives to immigrate to the U.S.:

- Husband or wife

- Unmarried son or daughter of any age

Application Process

In order to apply for a visa using family connections, the eligible U.S. citizen family member must file Form I-130. This form must be accompanied by proof of the citizen's relationship to the non-citizen. From here, the USCIS must approve or deny the immigrant visa petition. USCIS notifies the person who filed the visa petition if the petition was approved. USCIS will then send the approved visa petition to the Department of State's National Visa Center, where it will remain until an immigrant visa number is available. The Department of State then determines if an immigrant visa number is immediately available for the non-citizen even if they are already in the United States. The Center will notify the foreign national when the visa petition is received and again when an immigrant visa number is available. When an immigrant visa number is available, it means the non-citizen can apply to have one of the immigrant visa numbers assigned to them. Applicants can check the status of a visa number in the Department of State's Visa Bulletin.

If the applicant is already in the United States, they may apply to change their status to that of a lawful permanent resident after a visa number becomes available to them. This is one way to apply to secure an immigrant visa number. If the applicant is outside the United States when an immigrant visa number becomes available, they must then go to the U.S. consulate servicing the area in which they reside to complete their processing. This is the other way to secure an immigrant visa number.

People who want to become immigrants are classified into categories based on a preference system. You can find out more information on this preference system on the USCIS Web site.

OBTAINING A VISA THROUGH MARRIAGE TO A U.S. CITIZEN

The Legal Immigration Family Equity Act (LIFE Act) and its amendments allows the spouse or child of a U.S. citizen to be admitted to the United State in a nonimmigrant category. This visa class is considered K-3 and K-4, with K-3 being the non-citizen spouse and K-4 being the non-citizen child. This admission into the country allows that spouse or child to be able to complete the required processing for permanent residence while living within the United States. The LIFE Act also permits the spouse or child to gain employment within the U.S. while they are waiting for the processing of their permanent residency case.

Who is Eligible?

A person may be eligible to receive a visa under the LIFE Act if that person:

- Has a valid marriage with a U.S. citizen

- Has a relative petition (Form I-130)filed by the spouse, who is a U.S. citizen, of the applicant

- Seeks to enter the United States to await approval for their petition to become a permanent resident

- Has an approved Form I-129F (Petition for Alien Fiancé) forwarded to the American consulate abroad where the non-citizen wishes to apply for the visa

- Is under 21 years of age and an unmarried child of an alien eligible to receive a visa by complying with the above stipulations

Application Process

In order to apply to receive a visa through the United States, the valid U.S. citizen spouse must first file Form I-130 for the non-citizen. From here, the U.S. citizen will receive Form I-797, which is the Notice of Action form and indicates that the I-130 has been received by the USCIS.

The valid U.S. citizen should then file a copy of this I-797, along with a Form I-129F on behalf of the non-citizen spouse and any children, to the Service Center where the underlying I-130 petition is pending. Applicants should be sure to use the address listed on the most recent receipt notice or transfer notice and include a copy of that notice with your Form I-129F.

Petitioners should be careful to follow all instructions on each form and provide the Service Center with all necessary documentation. Following receipt of the Form I-129F, the petition will be forwarded to the applicable consulate so that the alien beneficiary or beneficiaries may apply to the Department of State for nonimmigrant visas.

OBTAINING A VISA THROUGH EMPLOYMENT

Obtaining a green card through employment is difficult and uncertain. Unless you are a person who is internationally known, a U.S. company must offer you a job that you are competent to do. In addition, for most jobs, the U.S. employer will have to advertise the job's availability and demonstrate that no qualified U.S. citizens or permanent residents have applied for it. The process of demonstrating that an alien is the only qualified worker available to fill an open position is called labor certification.

Who is Eligible?

There are four categories for granting permanent residence to foreign nationals based upon employment:

- EB-1 Priority workers:

- Foreign nationals of extraordinary ability in the sciences, arts, education, business, or athletics

- Foreign national that are outstanding professors or researchers

- Foreign nationals that are managers and executives subject to international transfer to the United States

EB-2 Professionals with advanced degrees or persons with exceptional ability:

- Foreign nationals of exceptional ability in the sciences, arts or business

- Foreign nationals that are advanced degree professionals

- Qualified alien physicians who will practice medicine in an area of the U.S. which is underserved.

EB-3 Skilled or professional workers:

- Foreign national professionals with bachelor's degrees (not qualifying for a higher preference category)

- Foreign national skilled workers (minimum two years training and experience)

- Foreign national unskilled workers

EB-4 Special Immigrants:

- Foreign national religious workers

- Employees and former employees of the U.S. Government abroad

Application Process

If you want to become an immigrant based on the fact that you have a permanent employment opportunity in the United States, or if you are an employer that wants to sponsor someone for lawful permanent residency based on permanent employment in the United States, you must go through a multi-step process.

- Foreign nationals and employers must determine if the foreign national is eligible for lawful permanent residency under one of USCIS' paths to lawful permanent residency.

- Most employment categories require that the U.S. employer complete a labor certification request (Form ETA 750) for the applicant and submit it to the Department of Labor's Employment and Training Administration. The Department of Labor must either grant or deny the certification request. Qualified alien physicians who will practice medicine in an area of the United States which has been certified as underserved by the U.S. Department of Health and Human Services are relieved from this requirement.

- USCIS must approve an immigrant visa petition, Form I-140, Petition for Alien Worker, for the person wishing to immigrate to the United States.

The employer wishing to bring the applicant to the United States to work permanently files this petition. However, if a Department of Labor certification is needed the application can only be filed after the certification is granted. The employer acts as the sponsor (or petitioner) for the applicant (or beneficiary) who wants to live and work on a permanent basis in the United States.

- The State Department must give the applicant an immigrant visa number, even if the applicant is already in the United States. When the applicant receives an immigrant visa number, it means that an immigrant visa has been assigned to the applicant. You can check the status of a visa number in the Department of State's Visa Bulletin.

- If the applicant is already in the United States, he or she must apply to adjust to permanent resident status after a visa number becomes available. If the applicant is outside the United States when an immigrant visa number becomes available, he or she will be notified and must complete the process at his or her local U.S. consulate office.

OBTAINING A VISA THROUGH THE DIVERSITY LOTTERY PROGRAM

Each year, the Diversity Lottery (DV) Program makes 55,000 immigrant visas available through a lottery to people who come from countries with low rates of immigration to the United States. Of such visas, 5,000 are allocated for use under NACARA beginning with DV '99. The State Department (DOS) holds the lottery every year, and randomly selects approximately 110,000 applicants from all qualified entries. The DOS selects the approximately 110,000 applications since many will not complete the visa process. However once 55,000 are issued or the fiscal year ends, the DV program is closed. If you receive a visa through the Diversity Visa Lottery Program you will be authorized to live and work permanently in the United States. You will also be allowed to bring your spouse and any unmarried children under the age of 21 to the United States.

Who is Eligible?

In order to be eligible to enter the DV Program:

- You or your spouse must be a native of a country that is eligible to participate in the Diversity Visa Lottery. You may also be eligible to apply if your parent was born in a country that is eligible to participate. (The State Department will publish the names of countries that are eligible to participate before each year's lottery.)

- You must have a high school diploma or the equivalent, defined in the United States as successful completion of a 12-year course of elementary and secondary education; OR you must have two years of work experience within the last five years in an occupation that requires at least two years of training or experience to perform.

- See the State Department information on the DV

program at the following Web link: **http://travel. state.gov/visa/immigrants/types/types_1322. html.**

Application Process

Before each year's lottery drawing, the Department of State will publish explicit instructions on how to apply in press releases and the Federal Register. Please follow all directions exactly. Millions of applicants are rejected each year for failure to follow the directions. Please watch the State Department Web site for more information on the Diversity Visa Lottery Program. Instructions are usually posted in August, and the registration period is usually held in October each year. You can find more specific instructions at the link listed above.

There is no fee for entering the diversity visa lottery. If you win, you must pay a fee for an immigrant visa and a separate visa lottery surcharge. Only the winners will be notified by mail at the addresses listed on their applications. Winners will be sent instructions and information on fees. Being selected as a winner in the diversity visa lottery does not automatically guarantee that you will be issued a visa, even if you are qualified. The number of entries selected is greater than the number of immigrant visas available because not everyone selected will be qualified for the visa or will choose to complete the processing. Once all 50,000 visas have been issued, the diversity visa program for the year will end. Please watch the State Department Web site for more information on the Diversity Visa Lottery Program. You may also call the State Department's Visa Lottery Information Center at 1-900-884-8840 for more information. Please note: There is a charge for each call. You may also contact your nearest U.S. Embassy or Consulate. A listing of U.S. Embassies and Consulates can be found on the State Department Web site.

OBTAINING A VISA THROUGH INVESTMENT

You may be able to obtain a green card by investing in the United States. If you are a qualified investor who is able to employ at least ten U.S. workers, you may be able to enter the U.S. with your spouse and children through the immigrant investor program. 10,000 immigrant visas per year are available to qualified individuals seeking permanent resident status on the basis of their engagement in a new commercial enterprise.

Who is Eligible?

Permanent resident status is available to investors, either alone or coming with their spouse and unmarried children. Eligible aliens are those who have invested — or are actively in the process of investing — the required amount of capital into a new commercial enterprise that they have established. They must further demonstrate that this investment will benefit the United States economy and create the requisite number of full-time jobs for qualified persons within the United States.

In general, "eligible individuals" include those:

- Who establish a new commercial enterprise by:

- Creating an original business

- Purchasing an existing business and simultaneously or subsequently restructuring or reorganizing the business such that a new commercial enterprise results

- Expanding an existing business by 140 percent of the pre-investment number of jobs or net worth, or retaining all existing jobs in a troubled business that has lost 20 percent of its net worth over the past 12 to 24 months

- Who have invested – or who are actively in the process of investing – in a new commercial enterprise:

    At least $1,000,000

    At least $500,000 where the investment is being made in a "targeted employment area," which is an area that has experienced unemployment of at least 150 per cent of the national average rate or a rural area as designated by OMB

- Whose engagement in a new commercial enterprise will benefit the United States economy and

- Create full-time employment for not fewer than 10 qualified individuals

- Maintain the number of existing employees at no less than the pre-investment level for a period of at least two years, where the capital investment is being made in a "troubled business," which is a business that has been in existence for at least two years and that has lost 20 percent of its net worth over the past 12 to 24 months.

Application Process

In order to seek status as an immigrant investor, you must file CIS Form I-526, Immigrant Petition by Alien Entrepreneur. The Form I-526 must be filed with supporting documentation which clearly demonstrates that the individual's investment meets all requirements, such as:

- Establishing a new commercial enterprise.

- Investing the requisite capital amount.

- Proving the investment comes from a lawful source of funds.

- Creating the requisite number of jobs.

- Demonstrating that the investor is actively participating in the business; and, where applicable.

- Creating employment within a targeted employment area.

Once the Form I-526 is approved, immigrant investors may obtain status as a conditional resident by filing Form I-485, Application to Register Permanent Residence or Adjust Status, if residing within the United States. In order to become a lawful permanent resident, eligible investors must file a Form I-829, Petition by Entrepreneur to Remove Conditions. Form I-829 must be filed within 90 days before the second anniversary of an Alien Investor's admission to the United States as a conditional resident.

OBTAINING A VISA THROUGH HUMANITARIAN BENEFITS

Immigration law provides several humanitarian programs to assist individuals who are in need of shelter or aid from various disasters and oppression, such as the following:

- Temporary Protected Status (TPS)

- Violence Against Women Act (VAWA)

- Asylum

- Refugee Programs

- Humanitarian Parole

- Victims of Trafficking and Violence Protection Act (VTVPA)

The following information will give you a brief overview of these programs; however, because these programs have complicated and lengthy requirements, you should visit the USCIS Web site for more in depth information on application processes, eligibility requirements, and necessary forms to be completed.

Temporary Protected Status

TPS is a temporary immigration status granted to eligible nationals of designated countries. In 1990, as part of the

Immigration Act of 1990, Congress established a procedure by which the Attorney General may provide TPS to aliens in the United States who are temporarily unable to safely return to their home country because of ongoing armed conflict, an environmental disaster, or other extraordinary and temporary conditions. On March 1, 2003, pursuant to the Homeland Security Act of 2002, authority to designate a country for TPS, and to extend and terminate TPS designations, was transferred from the Attorney General to the Secretary of Homeland Security. At the same time, responsibility for administering the TPS program was transferred from the former Immigration and Naturalization Service to USCIS.

During the period for which a country has been designated for TPS, TPS beneficiaries may remain in the United States and may obtain work authorization. However, TPS does not lead to permanent resident status. When the Secretary terminates a TPS designation, beneficiaries revert to the same immigration status they maintained before TPS (unless that status had since expired or been terminated) or to any other status they may have acquired while registered for TPS. Accordingly, if an alien had unlawful status prior to receiving TPS and did not obtain any status during the TPS designation, the alien reverts to unlawful status upon the termination of that TPS designation.

An alien who is a national of a country (or alien having no nationality who last habitually resided in that country) designated for TPS is eligible to apply for TPS benefits if he or she:

- Establishes the necessary continuous physical

presence and continuous residence in the United States as specified by each designation

- Is not subject to one of the criminal, security-related, or other bars to TPS

- Timely applies for TPS benefits. If the Secretary of Homeland Security extends a TPS designation beyond the initial designation period, the beneficiary must timely re-register to maintain his or her TPS benefits under the TPS program

An alien is not eligible for TPS if he or she:

- Has been convicted of any felony or two or more misdemeanors committed in the United States

- Is a persecutor, or otherwise subject to one of the bars to asylum

- Is subject to one of several criminal-related or terrorism-related grounds of inadmissibility for which a waiver is not available

Violence Against Women Act

Under the Violence Against Women Act (VAWA) passed by Congress in 1994, the spouses and children of United States citizens or lawful permanent residents (LPR) may self-petition to obtain lawful permanent residency. The immigration provisions of VAWA allow certain battered immigrants to file for immigration relief without the abuser's assistance or knowledge, in order to seek safety and independence from the abuser. Victims of domestic violence should know that help is available to them through the National Domestic Violence Hotline on 1-800-799-7233 or 1-800-787-3224 for information about shelters, mental health care, legal advice and other types of assistance, including information about self-petitioning for immigration status.

To be eligible to file a self-petition (an application that you file for yourself for immigration benefits) you must qualify under one of the following categories:

- **Spouse:** You may self-petition if you are a battered spouse married to a U.S. citizen or lawful permanent resident. Unmarried children under the age of 21, who have not filed their own self-petition, may be included on your petition as derivative beneficiaries.

- **Parent:** You may self-petition if you are the parent of a child who has been abused by your U.S. citizen or lawful permanent resident spouse. Your children (under 21 years of age and unmarried), including those who may not have been abused, may be included on your petition as derivative beneficiaries, if they have not filed their own self-petition.

- **Child:** You may self-petition if you are a battered child (under 21 years of age and unmarried) who has been abused by your U.S. citizen or lawful permanent resident parent. Your children (under 21 years of age and unmarried), including those who may not have been abused, may be included on your petition as derivative beneficiaries.

To self-petition, you must complete and file USCIS

Form I-360 and include all supporting documentation. Self-petitions are filed with the Vermont Service Center and should be sent by certified return receipt mail (or any other method providing assurance of receipt). You can find more information on the application process and specific eligibility requirements on the USCIS Web site.

Asylum

Asylum is a form of protection that allows individuals who are in the United States to remain here, provided that they meet the definition of a refugee and are not barred from either applying for or being granted asylum, and eventually to adjust their status to lawful permanent resident.

Every year, thousands of people come to the United States in need of protection because they have been persecuted or fear they will be persecuted on account of their race, religion, nationality, membership in a particular social group, or political opinion. Those found eligible for asylum are permitted to remain in the United States.

Unlike the U.S. Refugee Program, which provides protection to refugees by bringing them to the United States for resettlement, the U.S. Asylum Program provides protection to qualified refugees who are already in the United States or are seeking entry into the United States at a port of entry. Asylum-seekers may apply for asylum in the United States regardless of their countries of origin. There are no quotas on the number of individuals who may be granted asylum each year (with the exception of individuals whose claims are based solely on persecution for resistance to coercive population control measures).

To apply for asylum in the United States, you may ask for asylum at a port-of-entry (airport, seaport, or border crossing), or file Form I-589, Application for Asylum and for Withholding of Removal, at the appropriate Service Center within one year of your arrival in the United States. You may apply for asylum regardless of your immigration status, whether you are in the United States legally or illegally.

You must apply for asylum within one year of your last arrival in the United States, but you may apply for asylum later than one year if there are changed circumstances that materially affect your eligibility for asylum or extraordinary circumstances directly related to your failure to file within one year.

Refugee Programs

Every year millions of people around the world are displaced by war, famine, and civil and political unrest. Others are forced to flee their countries in order to escape the risk of death and torture at the hands of persecutors. The United States works with other governmental, international, and private organizations to provide food, health care, and shelter to millions of refugees throughout the world. In addition, the United States considers persons for resettlement to the U.S. as refugees. Those admitted must be of special humanitarian concern and demonstrate that they were persecuted, or have a well-founded fear of persecution on account of race, religion, nationality, political opinion, or membership in a particular social group.

Each year, the State Department prepares a Report to Congress on proposed refugee admissions, and then the U.S. President consults with Congress and establishes the proposed ceilings for refugee admissions for the fiscal year.

Eligibility for consideration is governed by a system of processing priorities. Refugees may be eligible for an interview for resettlement in the United States if:

- The United Nations High Commissioner for Refugees or the U.S. embassy refers them to the United States for resettlement.

- They are members of specified groups with special characteristics in certain countries as determined periodically by the United States government. (For some groups, only those with relatives in the United States are eligible.)

If you believe that you are in need of protection, you may wish to make your concern known to the UNHCR or to an international non-profit voluntary agency. If either of these organizations is unavailable to you, you should contact the nearest U.S. Embassy or consulate. Where appropriate, a representative from one of these organizations will discuss your situation with you to find out if you are eligible to apply for resettlement in the United States. If so, you must then complete a packet of forms, and the USCIS will conduct a formal interview with you to determine if you qualify for refugee status. If the USCIS determines that you should be resettled in the United States as a refugee, the U.S. State Department, together with other organizations, will then complete your processing. There are no application fees.

To qualify as a refugee, you must be able to prove that you meet the Immigration and Nationality Act's definition of refugee. Generally, refugees are people who were persecuted in their homelands or have a well-founded fear of persecution there on account of race, religion, nationality, membership in a particular social group, or political opinion.

Humanitarian Parole

The Secretary of the Department of Homeland Security may, in his discretion, parole into the United States temporarily, under such conditions as he may prescribe on a case-by-case basis, for urgent humanitarian reasons or significant public benefit, any alien applying for entry to the United States.

Humanitarian Parole cannot be used to circumvent normal visa-issuing procedures, nor as an instrument to bypass preference immigrant visa availability or processing for refugee status. Absent urgent circumstances, unless all other legal immigration avenues (such as applying for a non-immigrant visa) have first been exhausted by an alien, parole will not be approved. Parole is an extraordinary measure, sparingly used to bring an otherwise inadmissible alien into the United States for a temporary period of time due to a very compelling emergency. Note that Humanitarian Parole can only be requested for persons who are outside of the U.S.

A request for humanitarian parole may be submitted by anyone on Form I-131 Application for Travel Document. There is a filing fee for filing applications for humanitarian parole. Additionally, Form I-134 Affidavit of Support is also required to assure that the applicant will not become a public charge.

Victims of Trafficking and Violence Protection Act of 2000

Congress passed the Victims of Trafficking and Violence Protection Act of 2000 (VTVPA) in order to provide:

- Individuals who have been victimized in the most severe fashion with the ability to remain in the U.S. (temporarily and in some cases longer) and receive federal and state assistance

- Protections for certain crime victims including victims of crimes against women

- Law enforcement agencies with a comprehensive law that will enable them to pursue the prosecution and conviction of traffickers

Those who may be interested in this information include:

- Victims of a severe form of trafficking and non-governmental entities who may be working with such victims

- Law enforcement officers so that they may better understand who is considered a victim of a severe form of trafficking

- The general public on how the U.S. Government will pursue traffickers of persons

RESOURCES FOR FURTHER INFORMATION

The following government agencies and organizations offer helpful information for people looking to obtain a visa to immigrate into the United States. Many of the forms mentioned within this chapter can be found online in PDF format at the following government Web sites. You can also contact these government agencies at the telephone number or addresses listed below.

- U.S. Citizenship and Immigration Services (USCIS)
  Telephone: 1-800-375-5283
  (TTY 1-800-767-1833)
  Web site: **www.uscis.gov**

- U.S. Department of Homeland Security (DHS)
  Washington, D.C. 20528
  Telephone: 202-282-8000
  Web site: **www.dhs.gov**

- U.S. Department of State
  2201 C Street NW
  Washington, DC 20520
  Telephone: 202-647-4000 (TTY: 1-800-877-8339)
  Visa Lottery Information Center: 1-900-884-8840
  Web site: **www.state.gov**

- U.S. Department of Labor
  200 Constitution Ave., NW
  Washington, DC 20210
  Telephone: 1-866-4-USA-DOL
  (TTY: 1-877-889-5627)
  Web site: **www.dol.gov**

- The National Domestic Violence Hotline
  Telephone: 1-800-799-SAFE
  (TTY: 1-800-787-3224)
  Web site: **www.ndvh.org**

- United Nations High Commissioner for Refugees
  Case Postale 2500
  CH-1211 Genève 2 Dépôt
  Suisse.
  Telephone: +41 22 739 8111
  Web site: **www.unhcr.org**

★ AMERICAN FACT: *THE LINCOLN MEMORIAL* ★

The Lincoln Memorial is a United States Presidential memorial built to honor the 16th President of the United States, Abraham Lincoln. It is located on the National Mall in Washington, D.C. The architect was Henry Bacon and the sculptor was Daniel Chester French. The focus of the memorial is the sculpture of Lincoln, seated on a throne. This sculpture depicts the President as worn and pensive, gazing eastwards down the Reflecting Pool toward the capital's starkest emblem of the Union, the Washington Monument. The statue stands 19 feet 9 inches tall and 19 feet wide, and was carved from white Georgia marble.

Source: http://en.wikipedia.org/wiki/Lincoln_memorial

6
★ FORM N-400 ★

Perhaps the most important step in your quest to becoming a U.S. citizen is completing Form N-400, the application for naturalization. You can find this form on the companion CD-ROM, as well as further instructions on completing it.

You will need to submit the naturalization application to the USCIS service center closest to you. You can find a full listing of service centers in Appendix B.

Take time to fill out this form so that it is accurate. Make sure that you go over it multiple times before you submit it to the USCIS. The application will include:

- A cover letter

- The form N-400, Application for Naturalization

- An $80.00 biometric fee

- A copy of the applicant's green card

- Two passport-style photos

- A filing fee of $595.00

COVER LETTER

The cover letter is not a formal requirement of the application; however, it makes it easier for the immigration officer to look through your application. You do not want to make your cover letter into an essay. It should be a brief overview of you and the criteria under which you are applying for naturalization. You may also want to mention the enclosed documents in the packet.

SAMPLE COVER LETTER

To: <Insert Name>, The Adjudicating Officer

U.S. Citizenship and Immigration Services

Sub: **N-400 application for naturalization on the basis of three years of continuous residence as a Lawful Permanent Resident married to a U.S. citizen**

Dear Sir/Madam:

I hereby request you to give favorable consideration to my N-400 application for naturalization. The following documents are included with my application:

1. A completed N-400 form

2. A check for $675 toward application fee ($595) and fingerprinting fee ($80)

3. Two recent small photographs of me, each with my name printed on the back

4. A copy of both sides of my "Permanent Resident Card"

If you have any questions, feel free to call me at any of the following phone numbers: Work: (xxx) xxx-xxxx, Mobile: (xxx) xxx-xxxx, Home: (xxx) xxx-xxxx.

Thanks and best regards,

John Doe

<Address>

APPLICATION FOR NATURALIZATION

The N-400 is a long application consisting of 14 parts. You will want to make sure that you use black ink and print very neatly. Failure to do this might delay your application. It might also be a help to have someone else look over the application before you submit it. This will make sure that the application is legible and that you have fully filled it out.

To fill out the N-400, you will need to meet all the criteria for becoming a U.S. citizen. You can find a worksheet to determine your eligibility on the companion CD-ROM. This worksheet will walk you through a series of questions to determine your eligibility.

Form N-400 also has a nonrefundable fee of $595, plus a $80 biometrics fee for fingerprinting. You will need to submit a check for $675 with your application. Send your application to the nearest USCIS center.

There are very specific instructions for the N-400 form, and there are also a lot of agencies available to help you fill out the form for various fees on top of the application fee. You do not need to rely on these agencies. A basic outline of the parts of the N-400 form follow. The specific instructions for filling out the form are supplied on the CD-ROM, as well as the actual form N-400 that you can print out and complete.

Cover Page of the N-400

OMB No. 1615-0052; Expires 10/31/08

**N-400 Application
for Naturalization**

Department of Homeland Security
U.S Citizenship and Immigration Services

Print clearly or type your answers using CAPITAL letters. Failure to print clearly may delay your application. Use black ink.

Part 1.† Your Name. *(The person applying for naturalization.)*

Write your USCIS "A"- number here:
A

A. Your current legal name.

Family Name *(Last Name)*

For USCIS Use Only

Bar Code	Date Stamp

Given Name *(First Name)*   Full Middle Name *(If applicable)*

B. Your name **exactly** as it appears on your Permanent Resident Card.

Family Name *(Last Name)*

Remarks

Given Name *(First Name)*   Full Middle Name *(If applicable)*

C. If you have ever used other names, provide them below.

Family Name *(Last Name)*	Given Name *(First Name)*	Middle Name

D. Name change *(optional)*

Please read the Instructions before you decide whether to change your name.

1. Would you like to legally change your name?   ☐ Yes   ☐ No

2. If "Yes," print the new name you would like to use. Do not use initials or ††† abbreviations when writing your new name.

Family Name *(Last Name)*

Action Block

Given Name *(First Name)*   Full Middle Name

Part 2.† Information about your eligibility.††† *(Check only one.)*

I am at least 18 years old **AND**

A. ☐ I have been a Lawful Permanent Resident of the United States for at least five years.

B. ☐ I have been a Lawful Permanent Resident of the United States for at least three years, **and** I have been married to and living with the same U.S. citizen for the last three years, **and** my spouse has been a U.S. citizen for the last three years.

C. ☐ I am applying on the basis of qualifying military service.

D. ☐ Other *(Please explain)* _____

Form N-400 (Rev. 10/15/07) Y

Part 1 — Your Name

A. Print your current legal name as you want it to be on your certificate of naturalization.

B. This section is for USCIS use only.

C. If you have ever used other names, provide them in the following space. Include your maiden name (if applicable) and any other names you have used.

D. Name change (optional).

Part 2 — Information About Your Eligibility

A. Check "A" if you qualify because you have been a permanent resident for five or more years.

B. Check "B" if you are a permanent resident, and have been married to and living with a U.S. citizen for three years.

Part 3 — Information About You

A. Are either of your parents U.S. citizens? You may already be a U.S. citizen if one or both of your parents became citizens before your 18th birthday.

B. What is your current marital status?

C. Are you requesting an accommodation to the naturalization process due to a disability or impairment? The USCIS will make special accommodations for you if you have a disability.

Part 4 — Addresses and Telephone Numbers

You need to report both your residence address and your mailing address, and all phone numbers.

Part 5 — Information for Criminal Records Search

It is advisable to seek legal advice prior to applying for naturalization if you have a police record.

Part 6 — Information About Your Residence and Employment

If you are unemployed and/or receiving public benefits, you can still become a U.S. citizen. If you are or have been employed, you will be expected to show your tax returns.

Part 7 — Time Outside the United States (Including Trips to Canada, Mexico, and the Caribbean Islands)

This section concerning absences from the United States is very important. You must have been physically present in the United States for at least half of your residency period.

Part 8 — Information About Your Marital History

If you got your permanent residence based on a spouse's petition, and you divorced or separated from your spouse shortly after you got permanent residence, the USCIS may inquire as to whether or not yours was a real marriage.

Part 9 — Information About Your Children

List information about all of your children, even if one or

more of your children is a U.S. citizen. Your children, or some of your children, may get U.S. citizenship when you naturalize.

Part 10 — Additional Questions

You will be asked 39 additional questions. Answer these questions yes or no. Answer them carefully and truthfully. To become a naturalized citizen, you must be a person of good moral character, and you must be loyal to the United States and to the principles set forth in the U.S. Constitution. These questions are designed to find out if you meet these requirements, and they will be asked at your interview.

Part 11 — Your Signature

Part 12 — Signature of Person Who Prepared the Application for You (If Applicable)

Parts 13 and 14 — Do Not Complete Parts 13 and 14 Until a USCIS Officer Instructs You to Do So.

BIOMETRICS

The USCIS charges you $80.00 for a biometric scan. This is a scan of your fingerprint and works the same way as the previously used fingerprint card. However, the biometric scan is digital and more efficient because it is easier to store and easier to process. Upon receiving your application, the USCIS will instruct you on where to go to get your biometric scan.

YOUR GREEN CARD

Make sure to take photocopies of your green card and submit those with your application. The copy of your green card proves that you are a legal U.S. resident. Do not submit your actual green card, because you need to keep that on you at all times.

FEES

The N-400 has a filing fee of $595.00 and a biometrics fee of $80.00. You will need to submit payment for these along with the form. The payment methods can be in the form of a personal check, money order, or cashier's check. You cannot pay these with cash. Along with the rest of your application, make sure that you make a copy of the payment for your files.

You may ask for a fee wavier if you are a member of the U.S. military or if you cannot afford the application fee. To be eligible for financial assistance, you must be receiving government benefits, such as food stamps, because your income falls under the established poverty line. You will need to submit proof of your financial hardship along with your application.

The USCIS will evaluate every application individually, so you may not receive a fee wavier. If possible, it is best you go ahead and pay the fees to prevent a delay in your application. Keep in mind that you may receive an application fee waiver, but you will not receive a wavier for the fingerprinting fee.

Please keep in mind that you will want to double check the prices for the application and fingerprinting fees before you file, in the event that they change. The prices quoted in this book are representative of July 2008.

ONE LAST NOTE

Make sure that you keep copies of your application. This will give you proof that you submitted the application and all parts if something were to get lost in the mail or in processing. You will also need to keep a copy because your interviewer may ask you questions from the application during the citizenship interview. It will be easier for you to practice and know exactly what you said if you have a copy of the application readily available for you.

★ AMERICAN FACT: *THE WASHINGTON MONUMENT* ★

The Washington Monument is a large, tall, sand-colored obelisk near the west end of the National Mall in Washington, D.C. It is a United States Presidential Memorial constructed to commemorate the first U.S. president, George Washington. The monument, made of marble, granite, and sandstone, is both the world's tallest stone structure and the world's tallest obelisk, standing 555 feet 5.5 inches. It is also the tallest structure in Washington D.C. The construction of the monument began in 1848 but was not completed until 1884.

Source: http://en.wikipedia.org/wiki/Washington_monument

7

★ THE INTERVIEW ★

One of the toughest parts of becoming a U.S. citizen is the challenge of the interview. You will go through the citizenship interview after you have made your way through the mountains of paperwork required with your Form N-400. Once the USCIS approves your forms, they will assign you a date for an interview with an immigration officer. Your interviewer will ask you a mix of personal questions about your application as well as questions about the U.S. government. They will be testing you for a basic understanding of the history of the United States of America, as well as testing your English skills.

PERSONAL QUESTIONS

The interviewer will likely ask you some personal questions about yourself. They will be pulling these questions from the N-400 application. You might find this redundant since you already completed the application and they already know the answers; however, this is an easy way for them to test your English skills on a subject matter that you already know. Answering easy questions will also break the ice and help you relax.

They will ask you about your background. Sample questions may be as follows:

- What country did you come from?

- What subjects did you study?

- Do you have a degree? Where is it from?

- What do you do for a living?

- May I see your employment records?

- May I see your marriage license?

- Where do you currently live?

These questions will be pretty black and white. However, keep in mind that the interviewer is trying to see how well you know English, so you want to be conversational. Your English does not have to be perfect, but you do need to show a basic comprehension.

The interviewer will also ask you some more personal questions that involve thought and comprehension. These questions may include:

- Why do you want to become a U.S. citizen?

- How do you feel about the U.S. government?

- What does the U.S. Constitution mean to you?

These are questions that you should put some thought into and have a basic understanding of the answers before you go into the interview. Do not memorize your answers, but be able to explain yourself clearly. Also, above all else, make sure that you do not lie.

ENGLISH COMPREHENSION

You will need to do more than just talk your way through the interview. Your interviewer will make sure that you have a thorough comprehension of English.

Your English skills do not have to be perfect, but you need to show a basic understanding, as well as good grammar, diction, and an understandable accent. These English skills need to only be good enough to function well within society, because you will have a job interacting with other English-speaking citizens.

The interviewer will probably ask you to read or write some simple sentences in English. He or she may also ask you what some of the words mean. The interviewer may also ask you to read parts of your N-400 application aloud.

Some sample sentences the interviewer may ask you to write may be something such as the following:

- I want to be a United States citizen.

- Today I am going for a drive.

- The boy has a big dog.

- She went to look for a job.

- She drives the green car.

- I am married.

Studying for the English part of the interview may be difficult. However, one easy way to study is to read aloud from a newspaper. You can also have conversations in English with a friend or family member. Watching television in English may also help you understand English better.

CIVICS QUESTIONS

The interviewer will also be asking you questions about the United States government and history. There are practice questions listed in the following chapters, as well as on the CD-ROM.

You will be asked 20 questions about the U.S. government and the country's history. The interviewer may have you say these answers aloud or write them down, depending on which area of English he or she wants to test you on. Generally, these answers are spoken.

Do not be alarmed. You do not have to answer the questions perfectly, meaning that you can miss some. The interviewer wants to make sure that you have a good understanding of the government and what it means to be an American.

INTERVIEW TIPS

While you should study for your interview, you need to prepare for the interview in other ways as well.

Tip 1: Arrive on Time

You will want to make sure that you arrive to the interview

on time. You may want to find the interview location prior to the interview so that you know exactly where you are going.

You probably want to arrive early to make sure that you find parking. You may also want to be early because you will have to go through security. Depending on how busy the office is that morning, security may take a while.

Tip 2: Dress Appropriately

You will want to dress appropriately. Do not show up wearing ratty clothes. Show the interviewer how much becoming a U.S. citizen means to you. Treat this interview like you would a job interview.

- Women should wear a nice blouse and a knee-length skirt or slacks. These clothes should be neutral or dark colors so as not to distract the interviewer. Do not wear a low-cut blouse or try to draw inappropriate attention to yourself.

- Men should wear a neutral or dark suit. A tie is optional. These clothes should be neatly pressed.

Tip 3: Be Prepared

Make sure that you have all the necessary paperwork. You will want to gather these documents, such as your green card, proper identification, and any other documents that you may need. Bringing a copy of your Form N-400 may help you be better prepared.

Some documents that you may need include:

- Pay stubs

- Apartment leases

- Marriage documents

- Membership papers

These documents will help you prove your standing in the community and your value as a U.S. citizen. While the interviewer may not ask for them, they are always good to have on hand in case he or she does.

Put together your paperwork in a file and make sure that you have it in your briefcase or vehicle prior to leaving. You may find yourself rushed the morning of the interview, so it is best to gather these papers at least the night prior.

Tip 4: Ease the Nerves

Most people are nervous when they have interviews. Your interview is not likely to be different. Remember, though, that your interviewer is a person and he or she is trying to help you become a U.S. citizen.

Treat the interview more like a conversation than an interrogation. You have likely rehearsed plausible scenarios with family and friends, so think of the interviewer as your buddy. He or she is trying to get to know you and gain a better understanding of why you should become a U.S. citizen. Do not let yourself become rattled to the point where you do not make sense. Also, do not find yourself cold and withdrawn without saying much.

Always start the interview with a smile. A smile will make the interviewer feel like you are at ease, even though that may not be what you are feeling at all. Take a deep breath before the interview begins and go with the flow.

Tip 5: Always Tell the Truth

No matter what you do in the interview, make sure to tell the truth. If you are caught in a lie, the USCIS can revoke your citizenship. This should not be a problem for you, as long as you have been honest at each step of the naturalization process.

If you have unknowingly made a mistake in your application, such as leaving off a digit on your telephone number or not reporting a change of address, it probably will not cost you your citizenship. However, if you realize the mistake, you will need to notify the USCIS with the correct information.

AFTER THE INTERVIEW

You will not know whether or not you "passed" the interview until much later. You will receive notice in the mail for your citizenship appointment. If you receive this, then you have passed and will become a U.S. citizen the day that you take the oath.

If you find that you fail the interview, you will have 90 days to do the interview over. However, if you fail the interview a second time, you will have to start the naturalization process completely from the beginning, including a new application and processing fees.

IN CONCLUSION

While a lot may be riding on your interview, you need not stress over it as long as you are properly prepared. The following section of this book will help you gain a deeper understanding of both U.S. history as well as the English language. Keep testing and preparing yourself up until the interview.

Once you have made sure that you prepared for the interview, you are likely to pass it with flying colors. Just make sure not to let your nerves get the best of you.

PART 2

HOW TO STUDY TO BECOME
★ A U.S. CITIZEN ★

★ AMERICAN FACT: *MOUNT RUSHMORE* ★

Mount Rushmore National Memorial is located in South Dakota and is a monumental granite sculpture by Gutzon Borglum (1867–1941). It represents the first 150 years of the history of the United States of America with 60-foot sculptures of the heads of former United States presidents (left to right): George Washington (1732–1799), Thomas Jefferson (1743–1826), Theodore Roosevelt (1858–1919), and Abraham Lincoln (1809–1865). The entire memorial covers 1,278.45 acres and is 5,725 feet above sea level. It is managed by the National Park Service, a bureau of the United States Department of the Interior. Tourism is South Dakota's second-largest industry, with Mount Rushmore being its number one tourist attraction. Over two million visitors travel to the memorial annually.

Source: http://en.wikipedia.org/wiki/Mount_Rushmore

8
LEARNING ABOUT AMERICAN
★ HISTORY & GOVERNMENT ★

To satisfy the requirements for U.S. citizenship, you need an understanding of the history and government of the United States. The major topics covered in this study guide are:

- Early America
- The Constitution
- Branches of the U.S. government
- The President
- Political parties
- Notable presidents
- Presidents since 1980
- The court system
- Major historical events in U.S. history

EARLY AMERICA

The Pilgrims

People began coming to America in the 1600s. Most came to escape religious persecution and to start a new life. The pilgrims journeyed from England to the New World on a ship called the "Mayflower." Most were given passage in exchange for agreeing to work for their sponsors for seven years. They landed at Plymouth Rock, Massachusetts in 1620. Their biggest fear was being attacked by Indians, but the native Pawtucket tribe was friendly.

The pilgrims built a settlement and survived through many difficult times. The first winter was very cold and harsh. Almost half of the original settlers died, but the survivors persevered and were able to bring in a bountiful harvest, in spite of all the obstacles. A day of thanksgiving was proclaimed, and the pilgrims celebrated their first harvest with their Native American friends. This was the first Thanksgiving, and it began a tradition. Now all Americans celebrate this holiday each November.

The Colonies

People came from several nations in the 1600s to create settlements in America. Although the colonists grew their food and made most of their clothing and many other items, they still had to depend on England for other goods and trade items. They still thought themselves to be Englishmen and felt they were under the rule of the English monarchy. The English Parliament decided to make the colonists pay special taxes on certain items. The colonists protested, and violence resulted. The relationship between England and America soon began to deteriorate.

The Declaration of Independence

In 1776, a number of important men met in Philadelphia to draft a resolution calling for independence from England. This meeting was called the Continental Congress. The group included Thomas Jefferson, John Hancock, John Adams, Robert Livingston, Benjamin Franklin, and Roger Sherman. Thomas Jefferson worked on a draft of the Declaration of Independence for three weeks. John Hancock was the first to sign the document. Congress adopted the Declaration of Independence on July 4, 1776. Delegates came from the 13 colonies to sign the document. Independence from England had been declared. The English monarchy did not want the colonists to become independent, and a war soon began.

The Revolutionary War

The Revolutionary War (the War for Independence) lasted from 1777 to 1783. General George Washington was the commander of the Continental Army. It was a difficult war. The British troops were much better prepared than the Continental Army. They had more supplies and much better equipment. The Continental soldiers often went without food and did not have proper clothing. General Cornwallis, the commander of the British forces, was surrounded at Yorktown in 1781 and forced to surrender. The war officially ended in April of 1783, when a treaty was signed in Paris.

The Articles of Confederation

After the Revolutionary War, the new nation looked for a way to effectively govern itself while avoiding what it saw as an unfair and harsh system like the one endured under King George III of Great Britain. They thought they had found a solution with the Articles of Confederation, which the colonists wrote as the first constitution of the United States. Drafting of the Articles had begun even before the end of the American Revolution, and the view that a weak central government would be best for an independent nation became a common theme throughout the document.

The Articles of Confederation was the first constitutional agreement made between the American states. It consisted of a preamble and 13 articles. After winning independence from Great Britain, the fledgling nation needed to create a stable system of government. The states were all very different and had a variety of cultures. The colonists had won their freedom, but there were many growing pains. The new country was large and spanned from Georgia to the border of Canada. In addition to the American population, which was primarily European, there were thousands of slaves in the South. Boston was the biggest of the New England cities. It was very different from Charleston in the southern part of the country. The population of New York was mostly English, but there were also many Irish, German, and Dutch who lived there.

The Articles of Confederation was created with the intention that each state would retain sovereignty while adhering to a loose alliance of equal partners. However, it soon became obvious that this alliance could not effectively solve problems or protect the nation from harm.

THE U.S. CONSTITUTION

The U.S. Constitution, written in 1787, outlines the principles that form the basis for the U.S. government and establishes the basis for a representative democracy. In 1787, a constitutional convention was held at Independence Hall in Philadelphia, Pennsylvania. A new constitution was written, and it was ratified by the states in 1788.

Preamble

The opening, or preamble, to the Constitution explains the purpose and the objectives of the document. The preamble emphasizes that the powers of the U.S. government come from the people of the United States.

The Bill of Rights

The first ten amendments to the constitution are called the Bill of Rights. This document clearly outlines the rights of citizens.

Principle of Checks and Balances

In creating the Constitution, the founding fathers felt that they needed to balance the power between the three branches of government, so they provided specific duties and powers for each branch. The system of checks and balances gives each of the three branches of government the ability to monitor and regulate each other. This system assured the makers of the Constitution that the U.S. government would not become all-powerful and would always be a government "of the people."

Implied Powers

Implied powers are powers delegated to the federal government that are not exactly stated in the Constitution, but are reasonably implied. These powers give Congress flexibility when it comes to carrying out its powers. An example of the use of implied powers is the right to acquire territory. Thomas Jefferson used the principle of implied powers to justify the Louisiana Purchase in 1803. The implied powers have changed over the years. The framers did not want to limit the new government with only the expressed powers. They wanted to provide flexibility to grow and adapt as changes to the political environment required.

The Unwritten Constitution

The unwritten constitution has come about through custom and usage over the past 200 years. It implies that there are ideas, actions, and concepts not actually in the text of the Constitution but that have arisen as a natural extension of its use. An example of the unwritten constitution is the president's cabinet. Vice President John Adams created a committee of trusted insiders to assist the president. This group of advisors has become known as the president's cabinet.

The Great Compromise

When the delegates met to write a new constitution, they were determined to create a document that would be acceptable to all the states. The primary conflict was between the heavily populated states, such as Pennsylvania and Virginia, and the less populated states like Delaware and New Jersey. The disagreement centered around the question of how power should be distributed among the states. The states with a larger population wanted to have more power than the states with less population. The states with less population disagreed. These states felt that population should not be a factor in determining power. A committee headed by Roger Sherman of Connecticut came up with the answer. It was proposed that Congress have two houses: a Senate and a House of Representatives. The states would be represented equally in the Senate with two senators from each state; in the House, representation would be based on population. This would give the big states more votes than the small states. This solution was accepted and became known as the Great Compromise.

The Federalist Papers

In 1787, after the Constitutional Convention was over, there was controversy about whether or not to adopt the Constitution. Newspapers presented many arguments, both pro and con, to the public. The Federalist Papers were a series of 85 essays authored by John Jay, Alexander Hamilton, and James Madison. These papers were written to persuade the people of New York to approve the document and to promote the idea that the U.S. should create a government with three branches, each with separate powers. The series of articles eventually became known as the Federalist Papers.

The authors sought to explain the benefits of the proposed Constitution to the people and to defend it against critics. Some people were worried that the Constitution would give the central government too much power. Hamilton, Jay, and Madison tried to convince the people that a stronger central government would be more defensive of their individual rights. The Federalist Papers provided clear justification for the choices made at the Constitutional Convention and persuaded citizens that the government could provide greater protection for the people by placing less power in their hands. Today, federal judges frequently use the Federalist Papers when interpreting the constitution because it shows insight into the intentions of the authors.

THREE BRANCHES OF THE U.S. GOVERNMENT

The government has three branches: executive, judicial, and legislative. Each section of the government has certain powers that belong only to that branch. This prevents any person or group from becoming too powerful. If one person or group gains too much authority, the rights of citizens might be in jeopardy.

The Legislative Branch

The Legislative branch of the government is Congress. Article I of the Constitution establishes the legislative or law-making branch of government. It has two branches — the Senate and the House of Representatives — as well as agencies that support Congress.

The Senate is based on equal representation. This means that there are two senators from each state. The House of Representatives is based on proportional representation, which means that the number of representatives is based on the population of each state. The main job of Congress is to compose, debate, and create bills that then go to the president's desk to await his approval or veto. Congress also examines important issues of national concern and provides supervision of the executive and judicial arms of the government.

The Executive Branch

The executive branch includes the office of the president. It is the law-enforcing part of the government. This arm of the government is responsible for the daily running of the country. It does this through various departments, agencies, bureaus, commissions, committees, and offices.

The executive branch of the government is responsible for enforcing the laws of the land. The president, vice president, department heads (cabinet members), and heads of independent agencies carry out this mission.

The Judicial Branch

The Judicial branch includes the federal court system. This part of the government decides on the meaning of laws. It is independent of the executive branch and can declare a president's actions to be unconstitutional. The Supreme Court is the head of the judicial branch. It is the highest court in the land.

Courts decide arguments about the meaning of laws and how they are applied. They also decide if laws violate the Constitution — this is known as judicial review, and it is how federal courts provide checks and balances on the legislative and executive branches.

THE PRESIDENT

The president of the United States is one of the most commanding officials on the globe. His powers are granted by the constitution. The Constitution also limits the president's authority. His decisions and actions are always governed by a system of checks and balances. The president is chief executor and the commander in chief. He also has judicial powers. As chief executor, the president implements the tenets of the Constitution, enforces the laws instituted by Congress, and selects government officials. However, the president's acts are constrained by the other levels of government. The Constitution states that a candidate for president must be a natural-born citizen of the United States, at least 35 years of age, and a resident of the U.S. for at least 14 years.

Powers and Limitations of the Presidency

As commander in chief, the president is in command of the armed forces. He chooses the top military men and advises them. He may also send the armed forces into action in case of trouble within the United States and foreign domains. However, the president cannot consign U.S. soldiers to areas of international discord for more than 90 days without an actual declaration of war; this is a power given to Congress. The president uses his judicial powers to grant pardons and to appoint federal judges. The judicial authority of the president is regulated, because all of his appointments must be approved by the Senate.

The President's Cabinet

The tradition of the cabinet dates back to the beginnings of the presidency itself. One of the principal purposes of the cabinet — drawn from Article II, Section 2 of the Constitution — is to advise the president on any subject he may require relating to the duties of their respective offices. The cabinet includes the vice president and the heads of 15 executive departments: the Secretaries of Agriculture, Commerce, Defense, Education, Energy, Health and Human Services, Homeland Security, Housing and Urban Development, Interior, Justice, Labor, State, Transportation, Treasury, and Veterans Affairs. Under President George W. Bush, cabinet-level rank also has been accorded to the administrator of the Environmental Protection Agency; the director of the Office of Management and Budget; the director of the National Drug Control Policy; and the U.S. Trade Representative.

The White House

The White House is the official residence of the president of the United States. It is located at 1600 Pennsylvania Avenue in Washington, D.C. The White House has prevailed as a symbol of the presidency, the government, and the American people for over two centuries. In the winter of 1800, John Adams and his wife Abigail arrived in Washington, D.C. and became the first tenants of the White House. Since then, a succession of presidential families have moved in and out of the house. Each family garnered an abundance of lessons and memories from their stint in the White House, and each, in turn, left a legacy — an indelible imprint for posterity.

POLITICAL PARTIES IN THE U.S.

A political party is a group of voters who want to influence government decision-making by choosing and nominating members for public office. Party members usually have many ideas in common about running the government. They select people who support their ideas and try to convince voters to back their party's candidate.

The United States has a two-party system. A two-party system is one in which one of two political parties is likely to win an election and therefore hold political power. The Democratic Party and the Republican Party have been the two major political parties in the United States for many years. The

Republican Party was created in 1854. The first Democratic president was Thomas Jefferson, who presided from 1801 to 1809. The first Republican president was Abraham Lincoln, who served from 1861 to 1865.

Although the Democratic Party is the larger of the two major political parties, both the Republicans and the Democrats have many supporters all over the nation. The Socialist Party, Progressives, and Populists are some examples of minor parties that have existed in the United States through the years.

Although minor parties seldom win elections, they do often challenge the major parties. When a minor party gathers enough strength to be a serious contender, it is called a third party. A third party can win many votes and even influence the outcome of a national election.

Not all candidates for office run as members of a political party. Candidates sometimes run as independents. They build their own campaign organizations. These are sometimes called grass-roots campaigns.

NOTABLE U.S. PRESIDENTS

George Washington

George Washington was our first president. He is called "the father of our country." Washington was born February 22, 1732 in Westmoreland County, Virginia to a family of wealthy plantation owners. He married a widow, Martha Custis, and managed his land until the beginning of the American Revolution. When the Second Continental Congress assembled in Philadelphia in May 1775, Washington, one of the Virginia delegates, was elected commander in chief of the Continental Army. On July 3, 1775, at Cambridge, Massachusetts, he took command of his ill-trained troops and embarked upon a war that was to last six grueling years. After many battles, he forced the surrender of Cornwallis at Yorktown.

Washington wanted to retire, but he soon realized that the nation under its Articles of Confederation was not working very well. He became a prime mover in the steps leading to the Constitutional Convention at Philadelphia in 1787. When the new Constitution was ratified, the Electoral College unanimously elected Washington president. Washington retired after his second term in office. He died December 14, 1799 and the nation mourned him.

Thomas Jefferson

Thomas Jefferson was a powerful advocate of individual freedom and liberty. He was born in 1743 in Albemarle County, Virginia, to wealthy planters. Jefferson inherited thousands of acres of land from his father. He studied at the College of William and Mary, and then read law. In 1772 he married Martha Skelton, a widow, and took her to live in his partly constructed mountaintop home, Monticello. Jefferson was eloquent as a correspondent, but he was no public speaker. In the Virginia House of Burgesses and the Continental Congress, he contributed his pen rather than his voice to the patriot cause as the "silent member" of the Congress. At 33, Jefferson drafted the Declaration of Independence. In years following, he labored to make its words a reality in Virginia. Most notably, he wrote a bill establishing religious freedom, enacted in 1786.

When Jefferson became president, he slashed army and navy expenditures, cut the budget, eliminated the tax on whiskey so unpopular in the West, yet reduced the national debt by a third. Jefferson retired to Monticello after his second term. He died on July 4, 1826.

Abraham Lincoln

Abraham Lincoln was born on February 12, 1809 in Hardin County, Kentucky. He married Mary Todd Lincoln and they had four boys, only one of whom lived to maturity.

Lincoln made extraordinary efforts to attain knowledge while working on a farm, splitting rails for fences, and keeping a store in Illinois. He was a captain in the Black Hawk War and spent eight years in the Illinois legislature.

Lincoln became president in 1860 and held office during the Civil War. The deadliest war in American history, there were 620,000 soldier deaths and an undetermined number of civilian casualties. The war was fought between the Confederate States of America (Southern slave states who seceded from the U.S.) and the U.S. federal government, (the Union, or Northern states).

Slavery was a major issue of the war. Abraham Lincoln issued the Emancipation Proclamation on January 1, 1863, which freed the slaves in the South forever. Lincoln won re-election in 1864, as Union military triumphs heralded an end to the war.

Abraham Lincoln was assassinated April 16, 1865, just a few days after the war ended. He was shot at Ford's Theatre in Washington, D.C. by John Wilkes Booth.

Franklin Delano Roosevelt

Franklin Delano Roosevelt (also known as FDR) was born in 1882 in New York. He graduated from Harvard. Roosevelt attended Columbia Law School, and passed the New York State Bar exam in 1907. He married Anna Eleanor Roosevelt (his distant cousin) in 1905.

Elected in 1933, FDR was the 32nd President of the United States. He served an unprecedented four terms in office, until his death in 1945.

Roosevelt was president during the Great Depression of the 1930s. He is often credited with helping pull America out of the dire economic crisis. Roosevelt's New Deal program provided relief for the unemployed, recovery of the economy, and reform of the economic and banking systems. Programs Roosevelt initiated include the Federal Deposit Insurance Corporation (FDIC), Tennessee Valley Authority (TVA), and the United States Securities and Exchange Commission (SEC). These continue to have instrumental roles in the nation's commerce today. He is also known for instituting the Social Security system.

John F. Kennedy

John F. Kennedy was born in Brookline, Massachusetts. He graduated from Harvard and joined the Navy in 1940. In 1943, his Patrol Torpedo (PT) boat sank when a Japanese destroyer hit it. Kennedy was critically injured, but distinguished himself as a hero by leading his men to safety through dangerous waters. After the war Kennedy became a Democratic congressman from the Boston area and, in 1953, he became a member of the Senate. He also married Jacqueline Bouvier in 1953. In

1955, Kennedy was awarded the Pulitzer Prize in history for his book "Profiles in Courage."

In 1960, John F. Kennedy ran for president against Richard M. Nixon. At age 43, Kennedy became the 35th president. He was young and energetic and was welcomed by the country. Kennedy represented the possibility of a more prosperous future for Americans. He instigated many new economic programs, raised the minimum wage, proposed increased Social Security benefits, and encouraged Congress to fund a medical program for the nation's senior citizens. The White House was lively with the Kennedys' two young children, Caroline and John-John. No matter how busy he was, President Kennedy found time to laugh and play with his children. Jacqueline Kennedy collected fine art and furniture and restored all the rooms in the White House.

John F. Kennedy was assassinated in Dallas, Texas on November 22, 1963. Kennedy was shot and killed by Lee Harvey Oswald.

U.S. PRESIDENTS SINCE 1980

Ronald Reagan

Ronald Wilson Reagan was born on February 6, 1911, in Tampico, Illinois. In 1937, he became an actor and appeared in 53 films over the next two decades. In 1966, he was elected governor of California; he was re-elected in 1970. Ronald Reagan went on to become the 40th president of the United States, serving two terms in office from 1981 until 1989. His vice-president was George Bush.

Reagan is known for dealing skillfully with Congress. Reagan obtained legislation to stimulate economic growth, curb inflation, increase employment, and strengthen national defense. He embarked upon a course of cutting taxes and government expenditures, refusing to deviate from it when the strengthening of defense forces led to a large deficit. A renewal of national self-confidence by 1984 helped Reagan and Bush win a second term.

In 1986, Reagan obtained an overhaul of the income tax code, which eliminated many deductions and exempted millions of people with low incomes. At the end of his administration, the nation was enjoying its longest recorded period of peacetime prosperity without recession or depression. Ronald Reagan died at his home in Bel Air, California on June 5, 2004.

George Herbert Walker Bush

George Herbert Walker Bush, was born in Massachusetts in 1924 to Senator Prescott Bush and Dorothy Walker Bush. After Pearl Harbor was attacked in 1941, Bush postponed going to college and became the youngest naval aviator in U.S. history at age 18. After the war, he attended Yale University. He married Barbara Pierce in 1945.

Bush served as a member of the House of Representatives, prior to campaigning unsuccessfully for president in 1980.However, he was chosen by Ronald Reagan to be the vice presidential nominee that year. He served two terms as vice-president and ran again for president, this time successfully, in 1988.

Bush's Presidency is known for it's foreign policy. Military operations were conducted in Panama and the Persian Gulf.

The Berlin Wall fell in 1989 and the Soviet Union dissolved two years later. Domestically, Bush raised taxes and struggled with Congress. Bush lost the 1992 presidential election to Democrat Bill Clinton. Bush currently lives with his wife Barbara in Houston, Texas.

William Jefferson Clinton

William Jefferson Clinton (known as Bill) was born in Arkansas in 1946. He attended Georgetown University in Washington, D.C. After graduation he won a Rhodes Scholarship to University College, Oxford. After Oxford, Clinton attended Yale Law School and obtained a Juris Doctor degree in 1973. He married fellow lawyer Hillary Rodham in 1975.

Clinton was elected Governor of Arkansas in 1978. In 1992, Clinton was elected president. He served two terms in office from 1993 to 2001. Clinton became president at the end of the Cold War, and is known as the first Baby Boomer president. Clinton has been described as a "centrist". Clinton's presidency spanned the longest period of peace-time economic expansion in American history, including a balanced budget and a reported $559 billion federal surplus.

Clinton's presidency was marred by scandal, including controversy over real estate dealings and the Whitewater Development Corporation. Clinton also had a sexual relationship with a young White House intern named Monica Lewinsky, causing another scandal. In 1998, Clinton was impeached for obstruction of justice, but subsequently acquitted by the U.S. Senate. Despite these incidents, Clinton left office with an approval rating at 65%.

Since leaving office, Clinton has created the William J. Clinton Foundation, been involved in public speaking, and promoted global humanitarian work. He was also involved in his wife Hillary's failed 2008 presidential campaign.

George Walker Bush

George Walker Bush was born in New Haven, Connecticut in 1946 and raised in Texas. Bush attended Yale University. After graduation, he enlisted in the Texas Air National Guard. He married Laura Welch in 1977.

Bush served as the Governor of Texas from 1995-2000 and was elected president in 2000. He was reelected in 2004. Bush is the eldest son of George Herbert Walker Bush, the 41st President.

Bush's presidency was marked by turmoil beginning with the terrorist attacks of September 11, 2001. Bush announced the Global War on Terrorism and launched an attack of Afghanistan, and later, an attack on Iraq. Though the war was announced as a victory in 2004, the fighting continued and the war became very unpopular with many Americans.

President Bush signed into law a $1.6 trillion tax cut in 2001 and passed the No Child Left Behind Act in 2002. Perhaps one of the most critical acts that President Bush passed was the Patriot Act, designed to prevent terrorism.

Bush began his presidency with an approval rating of 50 percent, and that number skyrocketed to 80 or 90 percent after September 11. However, continuing war and a severe domestic economic crisis caused his approval rating to plummet to a low of 20 percent as he reached the end of his presidency.

Barack Hussein Obama II

Barack Hussein Obama II was born in 1961 in Hawaii. Obama graduated from Columbia University and Harvard Law School, where he was president of the Harvard Law Review. Obama moved to Chicago where he worked as a community organizer and civil rights attorney. He also taught constitutional law at the University of Chicago Law School. Obama married fellow lawyer Michelle Robinson in 1992. He served three terms in the Illinois Senate from 1997 to 2004. Obama was elected to the U.S. Senate in 2004.

Barack Obama has the distinction of being the first African American to be elected President of the United States. He was elected as the 44th President in November 2008.

THE COURT SYSTEM

The courts that make up the U.S. judicial system serve as a forum that allows two parties to bring their opposing arguments in front of an impartial judge.

Organization of the State Courts

Each state has at least four levels of courts: the lower courts, trial courts, appellate courts, and state supreme courts. The lower courts hear special cases, such as traffic violations; the general trial courts deal with all major civil and criminal cases; the appellate courts hear appeals from trial courts. The state supreme court is the highest court in the state system. The U.S. Supreme Court only hears the cases it wants to review. These usually involve parties seeking appeals from decisions of the federal Courts of Appeal or from the state supreme courts.

Selection of Judges

Although the president nominates persons to fill federal judicial posts, the Senate must confirm each by a majority vote. Because of this, presidents usually check carefully with the relevant senator or senators ahead of time.

The Role of Juries

A jury is a group of people who represent a cross-section of the community. They listen to court arguments and make decisions or recommendations about a case. They are an integral part of ensuring fairness in our justice system.

Judicial Independence

Throughout American history, the independence of the judiciary has protected individual liberties and prevented a tyranny of the majority. Judicial independence assures that each case will be decided on its own merits.

MAJOR U.S. HISTORICAL EVENTS

The Transcontinental Railroad

In 1862, Abraham Lincoln ordered the transcontinental railroad to be built. This extensive railway system ran from the East Coast to the West Coast and connected the countryside with the cities. Many immigrants from eastern Asia helped to construct the railroad on the western end.

The Civil War

In the 1860s, southern states withdrew from the Union and became the Confederate States of America. Lincoln believed the Union had to be kept together. He refused to recognize the Confederate States of America. Soon a war began. This war was called the War Between the States, or the Civil War; many men died on both sides. During the war, Abraham Lincoln declared the slaves free and issued the Emancipation Proclamation. In January of 1865, Congress approved the 13th Amendment, which abolished slavery throughout the country. The battles finally ended in April of 1865. On April 9, 1865, the general of the Confederate army, Robert E. Lee, surrendered to Ulysses S. Grant, general of the Union army.

The Fourteenth Amendment

In 1866, Congress passed the Civil Rights Act, which enabled African Americans to file lawsuits against whites and sit on juries. To protect these rights, the states ratified the Fourteenth Amendment and enfranchised African American men with the Fifteenth Amendment. In addition to these measures, Congress sent federal troops into the South to help African Americans register to vote.

The Great Depression

The 1920s was an exciting period in American history. It was called the "Roaring Twenties," and it was a time when most people were doing well. The stock market was up, jobs were plentiful, and there were many new and exciting inventions, such as radios, motion pictures, and airplanes. Unfortunately, the good times ended on October 29, 1929 when the stock market collapsed. Thousands of Americans had invested huge sums on Wall Street. The market suffered a huge loss and many people lost a lot of money. This was the beginning of what is called the "Great Depression."

During the Great Depression, the U.S. economy was at its lowest in history, and there were very few jobs. The Depression began in 1929 and lasted until 1940. It was a terrible time. Stores and factories closed, thousands of people were unemployed, and many became homeless. Herbert Hoover was president at the start of the Depression, and he felt that the only way to regain prosperity was to support the economy and have conviction that the situation would improve. Hoover kept saying that recovery was just around the corner, even as more and more factories and businesses closed. In spite of the increasingly difficult plight of most Americans, he did not offer government aid to alleviate their distress.

Americans became tired of Hoover's refusal to provide federal assistance, so he was not re-elected. Franklin D. Roosevelt became president in 1933. In the course of his first three months in office, he instituted many new programs that provided economic and agricultural relief. His "New Deal" reforms created jobs and initiated the recovery of the national economy. The New Deal went a long way toward making things better for the American people, and helped to instill a feeling that things were about to get better. But the economy did not regain its former strength until 1941, when the United States entered World War II.

World War II

When World War II first began in 1939, the United States was neutral. That changed after the Japanese bombed the U.S. naval base at Pearl Harbor, Hawaii on December 7, 1941. Many people lost their lives. President Roosevelt called it "a date which will live in infamy." This attack brought the United States into the war in western Europe and the Pacific. There were many important battles during World War II. One of the most significant was the Battle of Iwo Jima. U.S. forces invaded Iwo Jima, a tiny island off the Japanese coast. A picture of U.S. troops raising the flag at Iwo Jima became famous all over the globe and is now a symbol of the U.S. Marine Corps and World War II.

The Civil Rights Movement

The Civil Rights Movement was a series of protests and marches that ensued between the 1950s and the 1970s. For many years, African Americans were denied basic constitutional rights. Until the end of the Civil War in 1865, most African Americans were slaves. After the Civil War, they endured customs and laws that were designed to keep them from having the same opportunities and freedoms as other Americans. African Americans were prevented from voting or running for public office. In Atlanta in the late 1950s, for example, African Americans were not allowed to use the same water fountains or restrooms as white people. They were not allowed to stay in hotels or eat in restaurants that served white people. They had to go to inferior schools. This was a result of the "Jim Crow Laws," which were state and local regulations that were in effect in the South up until 1965. The social separation of African Americans and whites was known as segregation. The Civil Rights Movement was an organized effort to effect peaceful change, stop segregation, and gain equal rights for African American citizens.

Martin Luther King, Jr.

Martin Luther King, Jr. became one of the main leaders of the Civil Rights Movement during the 1950s. He was a Baptist minister and a nonviolent advocate of civil rights. King believed in peaceful protest as a way to change laws that were unfair to African Americans. He organized and led marches for basic civil rights. On October 14, 1964, King became the youngest recipient of the Nobel Peace Prize. He is considered one of the greatest leaders and a hero in America's history. He was assassinated in 1968. The assassination led to nationwide riots in more than 100 cities.

The Montgomery Bus Boycott

There were many protests during the civil rights era, but one of the most famous was the Montgomery Bus Boycott. It began in 1955 when a seamstress named Rosa Parks was arrested for refusing to give up her seat to a white passenger. When she was found guilty, she appealed her case. This was the beginning of the Montgomery Bus Boycott and a pivotal incident in the Civil Rights Movement.

The Civil Rights Act

Congress and President Lyndon B. Johnson responded to the Civil Rights Movement by passing the Civil Rights Act of 1964. This law prohibited discrimination based on race, religion, nationality, or gender, and gave African Americans many of the rights that Martin Luther King and other activists had been working for.

The Cold War

The Cold War was a conflict between the United States and Russia that began after World War II and lasted for almost half a century. It ended with the dissolution of the Soviet Union in 1991. Instead of guns, the weapons used in this war were technology and espionage. However, the threat of nuclear war from these two superpowers affected life on a global scale. Although there were many causes for the Cold War, a major argument between the two countries was over the political philosophy of communism.

The Bay of Pigs Invasion and The Cuban Missile Crisis

In 1961, the U.S. supported Cuban exiles in an attempt to overthrow Fidel Castro, Cuba's Communist leader. This military effort became known as the "Bay of Pigs Invasion." Castro's army prevented the invasion, and many exiles lost their lives or ended up in Cuban prisons.

The Cuban Missile Crisis occurred in October of 1962. It brought the United States and the Soviet Union (USSR) close to war over the presence of Soviet nuclear-armed missiles in Cuba. In May of 1962, Nikita Khrushchev schemed to place intermediate-range nuclear missiles in Cuba as a means of edging ahead of the United States in the development and deployment of missiles. He presented this idea to Fidel Castro as a means of protecting Cuba from U.S. invasions. The Soviet Union worked in secret and received Castro's approval to build the missile installations in Cuba. Photos of the construction were shown to President Kennedy on October 16, 1962. After a tense seven-day period, during which President Kennedy announced that any nuclear attack by Cuba would be regarded as an attack by the Soviet Union, the United States imposed a naval quarantine on Cuba. On October 28, Khrushchev announced that he would dismantle the installation.

Vietnam

The war in Vietnam was the focus of many of the major protests during the 1960s. By 1966, more than 500,000 troops were deployed in the area. By the time Richard Nixon entered the Oval Office in 1969, there was much opposition to the war. It seemed endless, it was draining the nation's military power, and economic resources. Nixon devised a three-pronged strategy to end America's involvement in the conflict. He began to gradually decrease the number of American ground troops. He sent Henry Kissinger, his national security advisor and secretary of state, to North Vietnam to negotiate a treaty. Finally, he authorized a massive bombing campaign in March of 1969 to target North Vietnamese supply routes. The war ended with the signing of the Paris Accord in January of 1973.

The Watergate Scandal

Watergate is a hotel and office complex in Washington, D.C.; it also symbolizes one of the most significant scandals in U.S. history. In 1972, several people broke into the Democratic National Committee headquarters located at Watergate. The FBI investigated and concluded that Nixon had been aware of the burglary and had attempted to hide the wrongdoing. Confronted with impeachment, Nixon resigned in 1974. Vice

President Gerald Ford was sworn in as president. Thirty days after Ford took office, he gave Nixon a full pardon.

Richard Nixon made many serious mistakes, but he will also be remembered for the good things he accomplished. He withdrew from Vietnam and achieved improved relations with China and the USSR. His actions reduced international tensions and decreased the threat of nuclear war.

The Global War on Terror

The Global War on Terror started with the attacks of September 11, 2001 by the terrorist group Al-Qaeda. Four planes were hijacked. Two crashed into the World Trade Center's twin towers in New York City. The damage from the planes' impacts was devastating to the structure, and the two buildings crumbled, to the horror of TV audiences everywhere.

Another hijacked plane was flown into the Pentagon in Washington, D.C. Though the damage and death toll was less, it still made an impact to Americans everywhere.

The final hijacked plane crashed into a field in Pennsylvania. Passengers struggled to gain control of the plane from the hijackers and it crashed into an open field, preventing the hijackers from targeting another building. In total, 2,992 people died on September 11.

The United States took action against the terrorists and launched the Global War on Terror, which began in Afghanistan to remove the Taliban and Al-Qaeda. The war was then launched into Iraq in an effort to remove weapons of mass destruction, which the government later discovered were not present.

9
★ ENGLISH SKILLS ★

An applicant for U.S. citizenship must have the ability to read, write, speak, and understand the English language. Sentences will be dictated to you to test your English ability.

PRACTICE EXERCISES FOR THE ENGLISH LANGUAGE REQUIREMENT

The U.S. naturalization test examines both your knowledge of American history and government and also your knowledge of the English language. The following sentences are examples of the type of sentences you might be asked to write during your citizenship test and interview. Please remember that the questions are examples only. Read the sentences below. Then have someone dictate the sentences to you, and practice writing them.

- She has a beautiful cat.

- He lives with his mother and father.

- She knows how to ride a horse.

- She found a very good job.

- He went to the grocery store.

- Her husband is at work.

- I went for a walk today.

- She bought a red dress today.

- I have four children.

- I am learning to speak English.

- Today is a rainy day.

- She is a good cook.

- He wants to live near his sister.

- My family lives in a big house.

- There is a big tree in the yard.

- The children go to school.

- The boys and girls play ball.

- The first U.S. president was George Washington.

- All people enjoy their freedom.

- America is the land of equality.

- Citizens vote in elections.

- The U.S. has three branches of government.

- There are 50 stars in the American flag.

- The Senate and the House are parts of Congress.

- Laws are passed by Congress.

- Congress can declare war.

- There are 13 stripes on the American flag.

Go over the sentences carefully. Correct your paper and rewrite any sentences that have errors. Repeat the above exercises until you are comfortable writing sentences when they are dictated to you, and you write them all correctly.

There are several common activities that an individual can engage in to learn English. An applicant can:

- Enroll in an English course at the local adult school

- Study with friends

- Complete practice exercises

- Memorize pronouns

- Learn the words that indicate feminine and masculine gender

- Borrow books from the local library

- Listen to language tapes

There is nothing burdensome in any of the above pursuits. They are all great activities that will help you learn English.

GENRES

The four genres of language are reading, writing, speaking, and comprehension. Some people are global, and can do each of these things equally well. Most people find that they are stronger in one of the above areas than in others.

Can you identify your strongest genre? You read, write, speak, or comprehend in your native language. In which area do you shine? You can use your strength in one genre to bolster the weakness in another. You will have many ideas of your own, but below are just a few examples that will show you how to use your strengths in one genre to bolster your weaknesses in other areas. If your greatest strength is in:

- **Reading** — You may feel more comfortable reading in your native language, but stretch yourself. Read a book in English, write a book report, and give the book report orally to friends and/or family, or record your performance to improve your speaking and comprehension. Remember, English only!

- **Writing** — Read what you have written. Write a summary and read it aloud to improve your reading and comprehension skills.

- **Speaking** — Write a speech in English, read it into a tape recorder, and listen as you play it back to improve your reading, writing, and comprehension.

- **Comprehension (listening and understanding)** — Listen to a recorded book, write a detailed summary of it, and read the summary out loud to improve your reading, writing, and speaking skills.

VOCABULARY EXERCISE

Arrange the following list of words in alphabetical order. Look up each in the dictionary and write the definition in your own words:

- America
- February
- Abraham Lincoln
- Washington
- Citizen
- Civil
- Congress
- September
- Country
- Mexico
- November
- Vote
- Liberty
- Rights
- United States
- President
- Memorial
- Flag
- George Washington
- Independence
- Senate
- Labor Day
- Columbus
- October
- Thanksgiving
- Freedom
- Register
- Senator

- White House
- Citizenship
- Privileges
- Bill of Rights
- Government
- Holidays
- Natives

- Naturalization
- Responsibilities
- Civics
- Election
- People
- Indians
- Supreme Court

Is there life after the oath? You bet there is. An applicant for U.S. citizenship does not necessarily need to be fluent in English, but he or she must have the ability to read, write, speak, and understand the basics of the English language. Why stop there? You will be living in the United States. It is to be your home. People in the United States speak a variety of languages and dialects, but the primary language used in the U.S. is English. You will have to study for the test anyway. After you become a naturalized citizen, you will still be learning the language and culture of America, but you will also be focusing on many other things. Right now, while you are budgeting the time to study for your citizenship test is the best time to focus on learning English. It is to your benefit to become fluent — or as close to fluent as time allows — before you take the citizenship test.

You live in a highly global environment, and everybody needs to be fluent in at least two languages. Learning the English language can, and should, be fun, and the more English you learn now, the easier your adjustment to the American culture will be.

10
★ THE U.S. CONSTITUTION ★

An applicant for naturalization is required to have a basic understanding of the principles of the U.S. Constitution. This chapter provides an overview of the U.S. Constitution; however, you can find the full version of the U.S. Constitution as well as Constitutional amendments in Appendixes G and H.

PRINCIPLES OF THE U.S. CONSTITUTION

The U.S. Constitution, written in 1787, outlines the fundamental ideals of the United States and defines the scope and function of the U.S. government. The government created by the Constitution was founded on the consent, or agreement, of the people. The Constitution accords specific rights to the people who live in the United States and gives certain rights to the government. The authority of the national government is limited to the powers written in the Constitution.

The Preamble

The introduction to the Constitution is called the Preamble. The Preamble states that "We the People" establish the Constitution. The U.S. government is actually a representative democracy.

The U.S. government is separated into three divisions: executive, judicial, and legislative. These sections of the government function under a system of checks and balances. The system is designed to ensure that the other divisions can check the work and activities of each government division; in this way, no government entity can become too powerful.

Bicameral Legislature

Congress is the legislative branch of the government. Congress is split into two parts: the Senate and the House of Representatives. This is called a bicameral legislature.

THE LEGISLATIVE BRANCH

The nation is divided into 435 Congressional districts. The residents of each district are represented by a member of the House of Representatives. People living in a representative's district are called constituents. Members of the House of Representatives follow public opinion closely. They are directly responsible to the people of their district and they usually agree with the general views of their constituents. Otherwise, they may be voted out of office. The number of representatives from each state is recalculated every ten years with information from the U.S. Census. If one state gains many residents while another state loses many, the first state could get one or more new representatives, while the other state could lose one or more.

Each member of the House of Representatives serves for two years. Senators serve for six years. The Senate and the House of Representatives check each other, to ensure that neither becomes too powerful. For a law to be passed on to the president, it must be approved by both the Senate and the House of Representatives. Specific powers are given to each chamber of the legislature. For example, only the Senate has the power to reject a treaty signed by the president or a person chosen to serve on the Supreme Court. Only the House of Representatives has the power to begin considering a bill that makes Americans pay taxes.

Federal Laws

The primary function of Congress is to make federal laws. Federal laws are rules that all people living in the United States must follow. Every law begins as a proposal made by a member of Congress. Most proposals can be initiated by any senator or representative, but proposals concerning taxes must begin in the House of Representatives. When the Senate or House begins to debate the proposal, it is called a bill. If the president signs the bill, it becomes a federal law.

THE EXECUTIVE BRANCH

The President

The president is elected by the people every four years. The framers of the Constitution wanted to limit the president's powers. Presidential powers include the authority to make treaties with other countries and to select ambassadors to represent the United States abroad. As head of the executive branch, the president names the top leaders of the federal departments. However, the Senate has the power to reject the president's choices.

THE JUDICIAL BRANCH

The judicial branch of the government is composed of many different federal courts. The Constitution created the Supreme Court, but Congress was given the right to create lower federal courts. Two examples of lower courts are the appellate courts and the district courts. Rulings handed down by lower courts can be reviewed and overturned by the Supreme Court.

The U.S. Supreme Court makes sure that laws are in harmony with the Constitution. If a law is inconsistent, the Court can decide that it is unconstitutional, and the law will be rejected. The Supreme Court has the final decision on all cases that have to do with federal laws and treaties, and on disputes between states.

When the Constitution was first written, it did not emphasize the idea of individual rights. Its goal was to build a government structure. A group of Americans called the Anti-Federalists wanted a list of things the central government could and could not do. In response, James Madison created a list of individual rights and limits of the government. For example, the list included the citizens' rights of free speech, freedom of the press, and freedom of religion. The list was in the form of changes, or amendments, to the Constitution. These first amendments were ratified in 1791.

★ AMERICAN FACT: *THE SUPREME COURT* ★

The Supreme Court of the United States is the highest judicial body in the United States, and leads the federal judiciary. It consists of the Chief Justice of the United States and eight Associate Justices, who are nominated by the President and confirmed with the "advice and consent" of the Senate. Once appointed, Justices effectively have life tenure, serving "during good Behaviour," which terminates only upon death, resignation, retirement, or conviction on impeachment. The Court meets in the United States Supreme Court building located at One First Street Northeast, Washington, DC.

Source: http://en.wikipedia.org/wiki/Supreme_Court_of_the_United_States

THE BILL OF RIGHTS

Amendments are additions or changes to the Constitution. The first ten amendments are called the Bill of Rights. They are a symbol of freedom to Americans and many others throughout the world.

The Amendments

- The First Amendment protects our freedom of speech and religion.

- The Second Amendment gives citizens the right to bear arms.

- The Third Amendment states that the government cannot force citizens to let soldiers live in their homes unless the country is at war.

- The Fourth Amendment gives citizens the right of privacy.

- The Fifth Amendment gives protection to people accused of crimes.

- The Sixth Amendment provides people accused of crimes with the right to a trial by jury.

- The Seventh Amendment gives citizens the right to a trial by jury to settle arguments over property.

- The Eighth Amendment states that the courts cannot require an unusually high bail.

- The Ninth Amendment recognizes the rights and liberties inherent in state constitutions and in state and local laws.

- The Tenth Amendment states that if the Constitution does not give a specific power to the national government, that power belongs to the states.

The 13th, 14th, and 15th Amendments were made at the end of the Civil War to extend rights to African Americans.

- The 13th Amendment ended slavery.

- The 14th Amendment states that all citizens have the right to equal protection under the law.

- The 15th Amendment guarantees that no state will take away a person's right to vote on the basis of race or color.

- The 17th Amendment states that voters from each state will elect senators from that state.

- The 19th Amendment gives women the right to vote.

- The 23rd Amendment gives residents of the District of Columbia the right to take part in presidential elections.

- The 24th Amendment outlawed the poll tax.

- The 25th Amendment details the process of succession for the presidency.

- The 26th Amendment lowered the voting age to 18.

The Constitution has been amended many times. Many of the amendments have been made to increase or extend the rights of Americans and to limit the power of the national government.

★ AMERICAN FACT: *THE LIBERTY BELL* ★

The Liberty Bell, in Philadelphia, Pennsylvania, is a bell that has served as one of the most prominent symbols of the American Revolutionary War. It is a familiar symbol of independence within the United States and an icon of liberty and justice. According to tradition, its most famous ringing occurred on July 8, 1776, to summon citizens of Philadelphia for the reading of the Declaration of Independence.

Source: http://en.wikipedia.org/wiki/Liberty_bell

11
THE NEW
★ CITIZENSHIP EXAM ★

The U.S. Citizenship and Immigration Services (USCIS) has designed 144 questions and answers for a new pilot exam. This pilot test was given to volunteers in 2007. The new exam emphasizes the principles of democracy and the privileges and responsibilities of U.S. citizenship.

WHICH TEST TO TAKE

A revised naturalization test was implemented on October 1, 2008. Out of 100 possible questions, the applicant will be tested on 10 questions and generally have to answer six correctly to pass.

Following is a 100-question test that you can take to help prepare you for the questions you will be asked in order to gain your citizenship. The answers can be found in Appendix I. Please note that these questions may not be verbatim, but they will help give you an idea of what you need to study.

Also realize that the immigration officer will be verbally asking you the questions and that you will not have a multiple choice option. Given this knowledge, a good way to study may be to have a friend or family member ask you the questions and you say the answers without looking at the various options.

You will also be able to find this test on the companion CD-ROM so that you can print it out and take it multiple times to help you prepare yourself for the questions.

PRACTICE TEST

1. *What holiday was celebrated for the first time by the American colonists?*

    A. Columbus Day
    B. Memorial Day
    C. Independence Day
    D. Thanksgiving

2. *Who makes the federal laws in the United States?*

    A. The President
    B. The Cabinet
    C. Congress
    D. The Supreme Court

3. *What is the Constitution?*

    A. Oath of allegiance
    B. The supreme law of the land
    C. The Declaration of Independence
    D. The Star-Spangled Banner

4. *What is the highest part of the judiciary branch of our government?*

    A. The Constitution

B. The Supreme Court

C. The President

D. Congress

5. *A bill becomes law when the President:*

A. Likes it

B. Reads it

C. Signs it

D. Vetoes it

6. *The Pilgrims came to the United States from which of the following countries?*

A. England

B. New Zealand

C. Egypt

D. China

7. *He was a leader of the Civil Rights Movement:*

A. George Washington

B. Abraham Lincoln

C. Martin Luther King

D. John F. Kennedy

8. *The Bill of Rights contains which of the following?*

A. The first 10 amendments

B. The last 10 amendments

C. The first 5 amendments

D. The last 5 amendments

9. When a change is made to the Constitution, it is called:

   A. A bill
   B. A privilege
   C. An amendment
   D. A responsibility

10. The Nineteenth Amendment gave women the right to:

   A. Go to war
   B. Have a job
   C. Serve on a jury
   D. Vote in an election

11. The leader of the Continental Army was:

   A. Robert E. Lee
   B. George Washington
   C. George Bush
   D. Abraham Lincoln

12. The war that occurred between the states is called:

   A. The Civil War
   B. The Revolutionary War
   C. The Vietnam War
   D. The Spanish-American War

13. The first U.S. capital was in which city?

   A. Washington D.C.
   B. Boston
   C. Philadelphia
   D. New York

14. Which of the following has the power to declare war?

    A. The President
    B. The Senate
    C. Congress
    D. The Supreme Court

15. When the President enters into an agreement with a foreign nation that does not require the consent of the Senate, it is called:

    A. An executive agreement
    B. An executive order
    C. An executive decision
    D. A treaty

16. How many members are there in the House of Representatives?

    A. 100
    B. 50
    C. 435

17. What do the stripes on the flag represent?

    A. The 13 original states
    B. The founding fathers
    C. The articles of the Constitution
    D. The justices on the Supreme Court

18. What is the street address of the White House?

    A. 1600 Pennsylvania Avenue
    B. 1601 Pennsylvania Avenue
    C. 1300 Pennsylvania Avenue
    D. 1700 Pennsylvania Avenue

19. *Who was the only U.S. President to resign from office?*

    A. Bill Clinton

    B. Andrew Johnson

    C. George Washington

    D. Richard Nixon

20. *The system of checks and balances incorporated into the Constitution ensures that each branch of government has the ability to:*

    A. Oversee the powers and actions of the other branches

    B. Limit the power of the federal government

    C. Limit the power of the state governments

    D. Receive a specified salary each year

21. *What are the duties of the Supreme Court?*

    A. To serve the president as Cabinet members

    B. To write laws

    C. To execute laws

    D. To interpret and explain the laws

22. *How many members are there in the Senate?*

    A. 435

    B. 102

    C. 100

23. *Which part of the government was created to respond most directly to the will of the people?*

    A. Senate

    B. House of Representatives

    C. The Supreme Court

    D. The President

24. *Who wrote "The Star-Spangled Banner"?*

    A. Francis Scott Key
    B. Katharine Lee Bates
    C. Irving Berlin
    D. Thomas Jefferson

25. *What is the term length for a U.S. senator?*

    A. 2 years
    B. 4 years
    C. 6 years
    D. Life

26. *The U.S. gained independence from which country?*

    A. Spain
    B. France
    C. England
    D. Russia

27. *Whose rights are guaranteed by the Constitution and the Bill of Rights?*

    A. All people living in the United States
    B. Registered voters
    C. The President
    D. Native-born citizens

28. *Which of the following is secured by the Bill of Rights?*

    A. The right to assembly
    B. The right to bear arms
    C. The right to a trial by jury
    D. All of the above

29. *Who is the current chief justice of the United States?*

   A. George W. Bush
   B. Samuel Alito
   C. John Roberts, Jr.
   D. Antonin Scalia

30. *Who said, "Give me liberty or give me death"?*

   A. Patrick Henry
   B. Benjamin Franklin
   C. Martin Luther King, Jr.
   D. Abraham Lincoln

31. *The Great Compromise provided for a (an):*

   A. Electoral college
   B. Bicameral legislature
   C. Executive branch of government
   D. National bank

32. *Which of the following is not a branch of government?*

   A. The legislative branch
   B. The judicial branch
   C. The executive branch
   D. The administrative branch

33. *According to the U.S. Constitution, a candidate for President must be:*

   A. A natural-born citizen
   B. At least 35 years of age
   C. Both A and B
   D. None of the above

34. **Who elects the President of the United States?**

    A. The Supreme Court

    B. Congress

    C. The people of the U.S.

    D. The Electoral College

35. **What do the stars on the U.S. flag represent?**

    A. One for each state

    B. The original states

    C. One for each President

    D. None of the above

36. **How many changes have there been to the U.S. Constitution?**

    A. 13

    B. 27

    C. 10

    D. 15

37. **How long is the term for a member of the House of Representatives?**

    A. 2 years

    B. 4 years

    C. 6 years

    D. Life

38. **One of the President's checks on judicial power is:**

    A. The veto

    B. Impeachment

    C. The pardon

    D. All of the above

39. *Martin Luther King, Jr. urged his people to employ which of the following tactics to achieve justice?*

    A. Using violence to bring about political change
    B. Using peaceful protests to bring about political change
    C. Moving from any community in which racism was practiced
    D. Demanding that reparations be paid to African Americans

40. *Independence Day in the U.S. is celebrated on which day?*

    A. January 4
    B. May 5
    C. July 4
    D. October 5

41. *When a court case is not a criminal violation, it is called:*

    A. A civil case
    B. A felony case
    C. A misdemeanor case
    D. An infraction

42. *Who was the 43rd President of the United States?*

    A. Richard Nixon
    B. George H. W. Bush
    C. Bill Clinton
    D. George W. Bush

43. *Which freedom is not protected by the First Amendment?*

    A. Freedom of speech
    B. Freedom of religion
    C. Freedom to assemble
    D. Freedom to Possess Firearms

44. *Who becomes the President of the United States if the current President dies?*

    A. His or her spouse
    B. The Vice President
    C. The Speaker of the House of Representatives
    D. The Secretary of State

45. *Who assassinated President John F. Kennedy?*

    A. John Wilkes Booth
    B. Jack Ruby
    C. Lee Harvey Oswald
    D. The Cuban government

46. *The disastrous invasion of Cuba in April 1961 became known as the:*

    A. Cuban Missile Crisis
    B. Kokomo Fiasco
    C. Bay of Pigs
    D. Vietnam War

47. *The first official U.S. government could be described as a:*

    A. Confederation
    B. Unification
    C. Monarchy
    D. Patriarchy

48. *How many terms can the President of the U.S. serve?*

    A. 3
    B. 2
    C. Infinite as long as he or she is re-elected

49. *In which city is the Liberty Bell located?*

    A. New York
    B. Boston
    C. Philadelphia
    D. Washington, D.C.

50. *Which of the following U.S. Presidents gave the Gettysburg Address?*

    A. George Washington
    B. Martin Luther King, Jr.
    C. Thomas Jefferson
    D. Abraham Lincoln

51. *Which of the following states was not a member of the 13 original colonies?*

    A. Georgia
    B. Vermont
    C. Virginia
    D. Pennsylvania

52. *How many states are there in the U.S.?*

    A. 49
    B. 50
    C. 51
    D. 52

53. *Thomas Jefferson wrote which pair of documents?*

    A. The U.S. Constitution and the Declaration of Independence
    B. The Articles of Confederation and the Bill of Rights
    C. The Galloway Plan and the Articles of Confederation
    D. The Northwest Ordinance and the Declaration of Independence

54. *What is the head executive of a state called?*

    A. Governor
    B. President
    C. Mayor
    D. Congressman

55. *Which was the last state to be admitted to the Union?*

    A. Hawaii
    B. Puerto Rico
    C. Alaska
    D. Washington, D.C.

56. The United States currently has two major political parties. Which of the following is one of them?

A. Republican

B. Blue

C. Federalist

D. Whig

57. What comprises the legislative branch of the government?

A. The President and the Cabinet

B. The Senate and the House of Representatives

C. The Supreme Court

D. The states

58. What is the supreme law of the United States?

A. The Federalist Papers

B. The Constitution

C. The Supreme Court

D. The Declaration of Independence

59. Where does the President of the U.S. live?

A. In the White House

B. In the Capitol building

C. In Texas

D. In New York City

60. How many senators does each state elect?

A. It depends on the state's population

B. 2

C. 3

D. 50

61. Which branch of government writes laws?

    A. Executive
    B. Legislative
    C. Judicial
    D. Administrative

62. How many stars are there on the U.S. flag?

    A. 13
    B. 100
    C. 50
    D. 25

63. Which President is referred to as "The Father of our Country"?

    A. George W. Bush
    B. Abraham Lincoln
    C. George Washington
    D. Andrew Jackson

64. Which country attacked Pearl Harbor during World War II?

    A. Germany
    B. Italy
    C. Japan
    D. Russia

65. Which of the following is not a color on the U.S. flag?

    A. Red
    B. Black
    C. White
    D. Blue

66. Which branch of government meets in the Capitol building?

   A. Executive
   B. Legislative
   C. Supreme Court
   D. All of the above

67. How long is one presidential term?

   A. 2 years
   B. 4 years
   C. 6 years

68. What is the name of the first woman Speaker of the House of Representatives?

   A. Nancy Pelosi
   B. Hillary Clinton
   C. Martha Washington
   D. Laura Bush

69. How many amendments guarantee or address voting rights?

   A. 2
   B. 3
   C. 4
   D. 5

70. What is the name of the highest court in the U.S.?

   A. The Court of Appeals
   B. The Supreme Court
   C. The High Court
   D. The Congress

71. Which amendment granted women the right to vote?

  A. 5th

  B. 21st

  C. 15th

  D. 19th

72. Who serves as the head of the executive branch of government?

  A. The President

  B. The Vice President

  C. The Speaker of the House

  D. The Chief Justice of the Supreme Court

73. The President's authority is limited by:

  A. The Constitution

  B. The First Lady

  C. The Vice President

  D. The Cabinet

74. One of the differences between criminal law and civil law is that:

  A. In civil law there is no plaintiff

  B. The government cannot be one of the litigants in a civil law case

  C. No one violated any laws in a civil law case

  D. None of the above

75. World War II began in what year?

  A. 1941

  B. 1939

  C. 1918

76. *John F. Kennedy was assassinated in which city?*

    A. New York City

    B. Washington, D.C.

    C. Dallas, Texas

    D. Brookline, Massachusetts

77. *Which of the following states did not attend the Constitutional Convention in May of 1787?*

    A. Georgia

    B. Maryland

    C. Delaware

    D. Rhode Island

78. *Name one of the purposes of the United Nations.*

    A. For countries to discuss and try to resolve world problems

    B. To settle civil wars

    C. To govern the world

    D. To protect the United States

79. *Who signed the Emancipation Proclamation?*

    A. Martin Luther King, Jr.

    B. George Washington

    C. Abraham Lincoln

    D. Thomas Jefferson

80. *How many Supreme Court justices are there?*

    A. 7

    B. 9

    C. 11

    D. 5

81. *Who acts as President of the Senate?*

    A. It is voted upon each day
    B. The longest-serving Senator
    C. The Vice President of the U.S.
    D. The Speaker of the House

82. *Can the U.S. Constitution be changed or amended?*

    A. Yes
    B. No
    C. Yes, but only by the Supreme Court
    D. Yes, but only by the President

83. *Who selects Supreme Court justices?*

    A. The American people
    B. The electoral college
    C. The President
    D. Congress

83. *In which month do Americans vote for President?*

    A. January
    B. May
    C. August
    D. November

84. *In which month is the new President inaugurated?*

    A. January
    B. May
    C. August
    D. November

85. *What are the first 10 amendments to the Constitution called?*

    A. The Preamble
    B. The Bill of Rights
    C. The Declaration of Independence
    D. The 10 U.S. Commandments

86. *Which USCIS form is used to apply to become a naturalized citizen?*

    A. Social Security card
    B. Form N-200 "Petition for Naturalization"
    C. N-400 "Application for Naturalization"
    D. 1040 EZ Form

87. *What song is the U.S. national anthem?*

    A. "The Star-Spangled Banner"
    B. "America the Beautiful"
    C. "God Bless America"
    D. "This Land Is Your Land"

88. *Who is the Commander in Chief of the U.S. military?*

    A. The Speaker of the House
    B. The Vice President
    C. The President
    D. The Chief Justice

89 *Which of the following is considered part of the judicial branch of the U.S. government?*

    A. Congress
    B. The Supreme Court
    C. The Cabinet

90. **What kind of government does the U.S. have?**

    A. A republic

    B. A monarchy

    C. A dictatorship

    D. A tyranny

91. **What is the minimum voting age in the U.S.?**

    A. 16

    B. 18

    C. 21

    D. 25

92. **Which of the following is a duty of Congress?**

    A. To make laws

    B. To enforce laws

    C. To interpret laws

    D. To explain laws

93. **In which year was the Constitution written?**

    A. 1800

    B. 1776

    C. 1787

    D. 1754

94. **What is the most important right granted to U.S. citizens?**

    A. The right to live in the U.S.

    B. The right to vote

    C. The right to happiness

    D. The right to live the American dream

95. *Who were our enemies during World War II?*

    A. Japan, England, and France
    B. Germany, Poland, and Switzerland
    C. Italy, China, and Spain
    D. Germany, Italy, and Japan

96. *What is the executive of a city government called?*

    A. President
    B. Governor
    C. Mayor
    D. Principal

97. *Which of the following amendments pertains to voting?*

    A. The 1st Amendment
    B. The 5th Amendment
    C. The 15th Amendment
    D. The 10th Amendment

98. *Freedom of speech is mentioned in which of the following documents:*

    A. The Bill of Rights
    B. The Emancipation Proclamation
    C. The Declaration of Independence
    D. The Preamble to the Constitution

99. Who signs a bill into a law?

A. The Chief Justice

B. The Speaker of the House

C. The President

D. The Vice President

100. Which of the following is a ship that brought the Pilgrims to the U.S.?

A. The Magna Carta

B. The Pinta

C. The Mayflower

D. The Santa Maria

★ AMERICAN FACT: *ARLINGTON NATIONAL CEMETERY* ★

Arlington National Cemetery, in Arlington, Virginia, is a military cemetery in the United States, established during the American Civil War on the grounds of Arlington House, formerly the estate of the family of Robert E. Lee's wife Mary Anna (Custis) Lee, a descendant of Martha Washington. The cemetery is situated directly across the Potomac River from Washington, D.C., near The Pentagon. More than 290,000 people are buried in an area of 624 acres. Veterans and military casualties from every one of the nation's wars are interred in the cemetery, from the American Revolution through the military actions in Afghanistan and Iraq.

Source: http://en.wikipedia.org/wiki/Arlington_National_Cemetary

12
★ CASE STUDIES ★

WORDS FROM THE PEOPLE

Case Study: Rebecca

"I acquired my citizenship by marriage, but still had to go through a lengthy naturalization process. You can't just get married and get citizenship. I was married to a person in the U.S. armed forces, and this shortened the process by a couple of years, but it still took me seven years.

You have to apply for permanent resident status, then once you achieve that and wait the appropriate time frame, then you apply for citizenship, and you have to be living in the same state for three months before you are eligible.

"It was frustrating at times because it's difficult to speak to an actual person when you have questions and they don't always have the answers. It meant numerous trips to the immigration office (never less than 1.5 hours away; at one point the closest one to me was seven hours away) for fingerprinting and various appointments.

"Also, on two occasions, despite me following the INS checklist to the letter, I was told I was missing photographs (that were NOT on the checklist). So, I had to leave the office and find a place (in cities not familiar to me) to get photos then return — this after I'd already driven a long way and had made every effort to be prepared. I pointed out to the INS office workers that they should make sure their checklists were up to date. It didn't seem to make an impact.

"I am English speaking, so no preparation was necessary for the language test. To prepare for the government exam, I printed out all the practice tests from the Internet and had my husband quiz me. I also took the online tests. As for the interview, I didn't do much to prepare. I knew all I had to do was answer the questions honestly and I would be fine.

"The most difficult part of the application process was the fact that the checklists were incomplete. Also, there's a limbo period. So when I went to get my driver's license in Virginia, I didn't have any valid proof that I was legal. INS would not supply me with documentation in between my permanent resident status running out and me taking the citizenship test. That was frustrating to say the least.

"I still have my Canadian citizenship. At least, Canada still recognizes me as Canadian...my permanent resident status ran out after I had gotten my date to take my citizenship test. The U.S. does not.

*"The greatest benefit you derive from being a U.S. citizen is that you get to VOTE! I recently published a book to thank the military men and women who afforded me this privilege. It was an all-volunteer effort. During my citizenship ceremony, the judge challenged us to do something to make a difference in our communities. I hope my book lives up to that. Please check it out at: **www.rebeccapepin. com**."*

Case Study: Bernardo Aguilar-Gonzalez

"At the time, I am not a U.S. citizen. I don't know if I ever will be. I am part of the Costa Rican Diaspora living here. I do have a son who is a U.S. citizen. At the time, I am a resident alien. I received my residence in August of 2005. Before that, I was an H1-B. I had been an H1-B since 1999. Prior to that I lived in the U.S. from 1989 to 1991  *as a J-1 graduate student. I had a B-1/2 for about 20 years. No cancellations. I am in a privileged minority of visa recipients.*

"I also received a Fulbright Grant for my grad studies in Georgia between 1989-1991, and I received a training leadership scholarship in 1985 from the U.S. Agency for International Development. I think that during the process of my residence, I have been privileged since fewer Costa Rican applicants receive visas than other nationalities. Even with this, I had to undergo the terrible inefficiencies and high costs of the legalities. The process of obtaining residence and even keeping my H1-B alive was full of inefficiencies and frustration.

"A process that is supposed to take three months will take 18. The procedure keeps you in a constant state of wondering if you are going to be expelled from the country any minute. You get quicker responses only if you pay expedited procedure fees ($1,000 or more). Even these responses take longer than stipulated in the notices you get. Your only access to them is overloaded phone lines where you cannot speak to a human being. All this was with the help of our HR department at the college. Later, with the residence procedure, we had to hire an immigration lawyer. This cost us $15,000, plus around $6,000 that the college paid for me (lawyer fees and immigration fees). The lawyers did have quicker access to responses and helped with the procedure.

Nevertheless, even then it was obvious this was an underfunded, overly bureaucratic, and obsolete model.

"Two cases: Once we all traveled to Costa Rica for a summer course. At this time, my spouse had switched from H2-B to F-1 in order to get her graduate degree in environmental politics. We both worked for the college during that summer course for ten weeks. When we came back through the Houston airport port of entry, because one requirement of her visa had been changed while we were out of the country, we were kept in the secondary room for around three hours without even being able to understand why this change was hurting us ex post facto. While in the room with our small children, we even had to be escorted by an officer to go to drink water at a water fountain. While in the room, we were able to see how other immigrants were shouted at and intimidated with strong remarks that were completely out of line by immigration officers. They were very clear in stating that they were gorillas assigned to make our lives difficult. The environment was completed by the fact that the toilets were filthy and had cameras in front of them. It was like going through prison.

"The funny thing is that you do not know if you are in the lines of criminals, or why you are being treated like you are. The environment got so tense that our children started crying. They were hungry and scared. After the change of guard, three hours later, a Latin American officer looked at our stuff, told us that he saw no reason why we were being held there and that we should go. So, in the end, the discretion of the person you are dealing with is all that counts.

"Once, while renewing our visas in the consulate of the United States in Costa Rica, our passports were stolen at gunpoint from the messenger of the embassy. At that time they had a system whereby you had to collect your passport from this courier private company so they could have fewer people waiting in the consulate. At any rate, it was their messenger — their system that broke — and in recognition of this they reissued our visas on new passports. They also gave us a letter explaining the situation. This was in 2000. Since then, several times while entering the country we have had to give explanations or go to secondary in order to clear out the fact that my wife's passport was used to try to enter the U.S. by some woman from Colombia who was caught and deported. Even as legal residents, we've had to wait long times for this to be repeatedly cleared. It was not until this year (2007) that we think it was finally removed from her record. So, we are hoping it will not come back again to haunt us.

"There are several more cases of our tortuous story, but in summary we think it is a broken system, designed today to highlight enforcement with lots of resources destined to the 'police' side and very little to the service. We know for a fact that many things are still moved from warehouses where paper files are kept all around the country because this institution does not even have fully computerized records. But we could prepare through the help of a service center that we run through volunteer work in Prescott College where we work. Well, following up with calls and the paperwork are ridiculous. We stated some of this above. I guess we are still in the process. My son probably will have it and I will probably apply for it in due time. Our concern is that coming from a country that has no army and also has more developed social services, we are on one side endorsing the existence, philosophy, and obligations of a country that has an army and we are losing the benefits of being in the Costa Rican socialized system. The main benefit is work. Yet, social and economic freedoms for the common citizen feel way more underdeveloped in this country than in Costa Rica. We feel that those are important. For me in particular, I feel no big gain in terms of freedoms in this country as compared to Costa Rica. I feel in loss. It is all about the job and the level of salaries."

Case Study: Mick

Mick obtained his visa in a lottery. "I was an illegal alien for seven years. I am originally from Ireland. I obtained my citizenship by naturalization. I 'won' my green card (a Donnelly visa) in 1993 in a lottery in which applicants were only allowed to send in one request. I then went through the whole

process of getting U.S. citizenship. Up until this point, I had spent seven years looking over my shoulder, dreading the possibility of even being pulled over for a normal traffic offense as that could land me in trouble.

"I prepared for the government test by memorizing the answers. I also had a friend quiz me several times before the exam. I do not remember preparing for the final interview, and it turned out to be a very pleasant conversation between myself and the INS officer. Before the interview, the questions that had been selected for me to answer seemed like the easier ones from all the possible options. In passing, I asked the INS interviewer if my perception was correct. Suddenly, he leaned back in this chair and took out another questionnaire from a different folder behind his desk, and said, "Here look at this one, we can also give people this one." This particular questionnaire had all the most difficult questions. I smiled and then returned the questionnaire to him. The interview to get the green card in the first place was the most difficult part. I had to fly home to Ireland to do it and I had to tell the truth in the interview… that I had been an illegal alien for seven years, had entered and left the country on many occasions during that time because of obvious loopholes in the INS process at that time, and that I had a business which served high-profile and famous individuals and which also employed U.S. citizens, none of whom knew my alien status.

"To be able to come and go freely from the U.S. is great. Also, I have 'used' the fact that I am a U.S. citizen on one occasion when my wife and I were entrapped in a police speeding ticket scam in eastern Europe. At first, the officer believed I was Irish and my wife to be Spanish, but as soon as I pulled out my U.S. passport, his tone changed dramatically and he suddenly created an easy way for us to exit from a situation that only seconds earlier had seemed impassible.

"On the day of the swearing-in ceremony at the courthouse in White Plains, New York, I was amazed at how many people were there with family and friends. But the event went much longer than I had anticipated. It just so happened that I had an important business meeting arranged in Manhattan that same morning. All I can remember after the ceremony is waiting in line to shake the hands of the judge to get my certificate of naturalization and jumping in my Porsche to get to the city! What a great country!"

Case Study: Ana Cecilia Bukowski

Ana Cecilia Bukowski acquired her citizenship by marriage in 2003. She said the process of naturalization was very easy. She prepared for the U.S. citizenship exam by studying on her own with a book. She did not really need to prepare for the English or interview segment of the test because she was already bilingual.

Ana found that waiting at the Oath Ceremony to be sworn in was the most difficult part of the application process. She does have dual citizenship in Costa Rica. She has found the greatest benefit from becoming a U.S. citizen has been the ability to vote in U.S. elections and voicing her opinions. She is also happy that she can choose government officials.

"In my native country (Costa Rica), I also enjoyed all the same freedoms I now enjoy in the U.S. But, being able to express my political opinion in the U.S. is important to me. While I was a legal resident, I always refrained from doing so out of respect for my new home in the U.S. and for its citizens."

Case Study: Sandra Patricia Molina

Sandra acquired her citizenship through marriage. She now has dual citizenship with the U.S. and Colombia. She was not required to give up any rights and/ or privileges from Colombia when she received her dual citizenship. She prepared for the citizenship test by studying 100 sample test questions.

Her husband and daughter helped her with the English and Interview sections. She found the most difficult part of the application process to be the wait for the oath. Sandra says the greatest benefit she has derived from becoming a U.S. Citizen has been her ability to vote and her freedom of speech.

WORDS FROM THE LAWYERS

Case Study: Evelyne M. Hart

Distinguishing Between Residence and Physical Presence.

Residence and Physical Presence are two different concepts. Residence denotes the grant of lawful permanent residency and the right to live in the United States. It is evidenced by the Resident Alien Card, formerly called the green card. Physical presence signifies how much time you have  *spent in the United States as compared to absences outside the United States. An applicant for naturalization can be absent from the United States 30 months minus 1 day and still qualify to apply.*

However, if a resident alien is absent from the United States more than 6 months and less than one year, he is infringing on his residence and may be asked to provide ample explanations that he has not abandoned his residency. If a resident alien is absent from the United States more than one year, DHS will generally treat that person as having abandoned his residency. The person may be granted SB1 category if she can show that her absence from the United States was for reasons beyond her control or if DHS does not see any benefits to barring the resident alien from re-entry. A re-entry permit will protect a resident alien from such problems.

N-400. Part 7. Time Outside the United States.

The eligibility worksheet (M-480, items 4 and 5) informs the applicant that she is eligible to apply for naturalization if she has not been out of the United States for half the time preceding the 3 or 5 years before applying. However, this is a trap for the unwary. Except for four exceptions , the applicant needs to be aware that trips outside the United States lasting one year or more is an absolute bar to naturalization. If the applicant has been absent from the United States for six months but less than one year, he must explain that he did not abandon his residency and provide proof to support his explanation. In both cases, the applicant may prefer to clear the slate and not provide explanations by waiting 4 years and one day from the time he returns to the United States to apply for naturalization again.

The Re-Entry Permit.

The re-entry permit does protect a resident alien from losing his residency. Contrary to popular belief, however, the re-entry permit does not preserve the physical presence requirement for naturalization purposes if the applicant has been outside the United States more than 6 months. The applicant would still have to wait the 4 years and one day or the 2 years and one day before applying for citizenship.

[1] An applicant is eligible to file for naturalization after 3 years from obtaining residency if he adjusted status through his U.S. Citizen spouse and he is still married to the same spouse.

[2] Exceptions: Military service abroad; certain lawful permanent resident employees who work abroad or are married to U.S. citizens who work abroad; the spouse, child or parent of a U.S. Citizen who died in combat; or the spouse of the person who was granted American citizenship posthumously.

[3] If the statutory 3-year period is involved, then the applicant need only wait 2 years and one day from the time he returns to apply for naturalization again.

LAW OFFICES OF EVELYNE M. HART
1440 N. Harbor Boulevard, Suite 800
Fullerton, CA 92835
Toll Free: (866) HART-USA (427-8872)
Phone 714-449-8409 • Fax: 714-441-2746
Web: **www.hartimmigration.com**
E-Mail: ehart@hartimmigration.com

Case Study: Kalish Law Office

I think that there are really three areas to consider when preparing to take the naturalization test. It can be easy to feel intimidated or overwhelmed by the idea of taking this test, especially if you have not taken a test in awhile. I tell my clients to take it step by step and here is what I think are the most important things to remember:

1. *Make sure your immigration filing is properly prepared. From the very beginning, be sure to be complete and truthful with your application and paperwork. Get whatever help you need in completing and filing your application. Be sure that the immigration service has your proper address at all times. These early steps will prevent anxiety later on.*

   If you have a disability, you may be entitled to special accommodation at the test. If so, accept the help. Don't try to be brave and "tough it out".

If your primary language is one other than English and you are entitled to an exemption to take the test in your primary language, don't be afraid to do so. Be sure that you think about these things in advance and file your request in time.

2. *Be aware of how you study best and take the time to do it. If you learn best by reading and writing things yourself, do that. If you learn best by having someone ask you questions out loud, do that. Many communities have classes or workshops at libraries and community centers for test preparation. If you are the kind of person who learns best in a group, find one. Use a good study guide to help you prepare. Also, look at the study materials provided free online on **www.uscis.gov**. Be sure to download and use the ones that will help you.*

3. *Prepare yourself physically and emotionally. Be sure that you get proper rest and nutrition for at least a few days before the test. Try to avoid last minute "cramming" or staying up all night. Pace yourself with your studying. Get yourself mentally prepared to have a great result. Wear clothing that is comfortable, but still makes you feel good. You should go into the test rested, comfortable and confident!*

Laura Kalish is an immigration attorney and a partner in the Kalish Law Firm in The Woodlands, Texas. She can be reached at kalishlawlaura@aol.com. The firm's Web site can be found at **www.kalishlawtexas.com**.

Kalish Law Office
25907 Oak Ridge Dr.
The Woodlands, Texas 77380
281-363-3700
www.kalishlawtexas.com

Case Study: Sonia M. Munoz

Benefits of U.S. Citizenship

The U.S. Immigration system is full of legal technicalities that can either present great risk or fantastic opportunities for those who understand the law. Unfortunately, many people assume that because the forms are simple, that the process is equally simple. For example, did you know that though  *you may still not be a U.S. citizen, your spouse, parent, or minor child may be able to obtain legal status based on your pending process?*

In situations where an individual has been a lawful permanent resident (Green Card holder) and is soon to qualify to start the application process for naturalization or has a pending naturalization application, there is immigration relief available to his or her immediate relatives. In these sorts of situations, the naturalization applicant's parents, spouse, and unmarried minor children are all able to seek legal protection through Deferred Action from the U.S. Citizenship and Immigration Services (USCIS).

Deferred Action is a discretionary relief granted by the District Director of the USCIS which grants the applicant legal immigration status in the U.S. along with eligibility to obtain an employment authorization card, commonly referred to as a work permit. Deferred Action grants legal immigration status to the spouse, parent, or unmarried minor child of a naturalization applicant during their wait for the applicant to become a naturalized U.S. citizen. It also grants them permission to work legally in this country by making them eligible to apply for a work permit.

Aside from the existence of Deferred Action relief, there are other benefits related to the process of U.S. naturalization. Many benefits of US citizenship relate to financial benefits available to citizens. Once someone becomes a naturalized US citizen, he or she can qualify to receive the following financial benefits:

1. Full Social Security benefits after retirement whether living in the United States or abroad. (Green Card holders are only eligible to receive a percentage of the Social Security benefits earned and must reside in the US to receive them).

2. Full government aid such as supplemental Social Security benefits, food stamps, and several available grants and financial benefits for college students.

3. More commercial and residential mortgage loan options and lower interest rates.

In addition to financial perks, a naturalized U.S. citizen can vote at federal, state, and local level and thereby make a positive difference in the government. In terms of travel, a U.S. citizen can enter and leave the U.S. without limit and will never have to worry about being subject to deportation even if arrested for a crime committed. Lastly, and most importantly, to many people, U.S. citizens are able to petition parents, siblings, children, and spouses from abroad and in many cases even grant derivative U.S. citizenship to their unmarried minor children. If you are uncertain as how to take advantage of the opportunities that may be present, you should discuss your specific situation with an Immigration attorney.

Sonia M. Munoz is the Managing Attorney of International Legal Counsel, LLC, a law firm located in South Florida exclusively representing foreign professionals and investors through all legal aspects of the transition to the United States including legal counsel on Immigration, Business, Real Estate, and International taxes. Visit the Firm's site to read published articles from Ms. Munoz regarding visas available to foreign national investors at **www.ilclawfirm. com**.

Sonia Munoz is a multi-lingual attorney admitted to the Florida Bar with experience in litigation and legal counsel, research and writing in both the private sector and the judicial system.

Ms. Munoz's passion, dedication, and talent have led her to become an active role model and leader in the legal community. She graduated with a Juris Doctorate with a specialization in International Commercial Law from the University of Florida Levin College of Law. Ms. Munoz also studied European Business Law at the Faculte du Droit in Montpellier, France, and the Universiteit du Leiden, in Leiden, The Netherlands. Prior to that, she graduated from the University of Miami with a double major in Psychology and Political Science with high honors.

In addition to working as a Political Analyst with a Top Secret Clearance from the CIA, Ms. Munoz has traveled extensively, having resided and worked in the European Union and for the International Court of The Hague in The Netherlands. She has co-authored a bench book regarding International law and its application and effects on domestic court hearings, conducted and participated in conferences with State Senators and Representatives, and interviewed former President Bill Clinton on a globally-televised program where she represented American college students.

Ms. Munoz is barred in several courts including State and Federal District Courts of Appeals. Her background as a

Judicial Clerk for the Honorable Chief Judge Stevenson in the 4th District Court of Appeals gives her a special insight into the Judge's view and considerations of cases. As a judicial clerk at the Court of Appeals, Ms. Munoz drafted appellate judiciary briefs and judiciary opinions for cases involving criminal, civil, and business law. Because of this, her extensive travel and cultural awareness, and her extraordinary commitment to ethics, Ms. Munoz is a fierce and vocal advocate for the rights of immigrants. She has been published in newspapers all throughout the US, and has been interviewed on local radio and television as an immigration expert.

Sonia M. Munoz
International Legal Counsel, LLC
110 East Broward Blvd., Suite 1700
Fort Lauderdale, FL 33301
Ph: 954-376-3767 • Fax: 954-246-3014
www.ilclawfirm.com

Case Study: Jennifer Lim

Applicants for U.S. citizenship should be aware that they have some judicial remedies available if there is any action by an officer of the U.S. government agency which can be considered as an abuse of their government authority. I recently represented a client in federal court, who had originally received  *his permanent residence in the 1980's and was forced to sign a form relinquishing his permanent residence by a U.S. consular officer while he was abroad in the early 1990's. At that time, this client was only a 19-year-old student who was going abroad to attend a culinary school for a couple of years. Due to the consular officer's ignorance of the applicable regulations, this client was forced to give up his permanent residence and given a tourist visa to enter the United States.*

Subsequently, this client remained in the U.S. after reentering the U.S., because of his extensive family ties and having grown up in this country. Later, the government even sent him a "replacement" permanent resident card. However, when he applied for citizenship through naturalization, the government denied his application and claimed he was not a permanent resident and therefore not eligible for naturalization, based on the form which he was forced to sign about 10 years ago. Subsequently, he consulted with me and we filed a suit in federal court for a de novo review of his citizenship application by the district court judge. In that case, the government admitted their mistake after the lawsuit was filed and the client was able to take his citizenship oath.

Jennifer Lim • Law Office of Jennifer Lim
123 S. Figueroa Street, Suite 220 • Los Angeles, CA 90012
Ph: 213-680-9332 • Fax: 213-680-9337
www.jenniferlim.com

★ AMERICAN FACT: *GEORGE WASHINGTON* ★

George Washington served as the first President of the United States (1789–1797), and led the Continental Army to victory over Great Britain in the American Revolutionary War. Washington's devotion to civic virtue made him an exemplary figure among early American politicians. Washington died in 1799, and in his funeral oration, Henry Lee said that of all Americans, he was "first in war, first in peace, and first in the hearts of his countrymen." Washington has been consistently ranked by scholars as one of the greatest U.S. Presidents. Statues of George Washington can be found across the United States, such as the one located in Richmond, Virginia, pictured above.

Source: http://en.wikipedia.org/wiki/George_washinton

APPENDIX A
COUNTRIES APPROVING
★ DUAL CITIZENSHIP ★

The following is a partial list of countries that currently permit dual citizenship:

- Albania
- Antigua and Barbuda
- Argentina
- Australia
- Barbados
- Belize
- Benin
- Brazil
- Burkina Faso
- Cambodia
- Canada
- China, People's Republic of
- Chile
- Colombia
- Costa Rica
- Croatia
- Czech Republic
- Dominican Republic
- Dominica
- Ecuador
- El Salvador
- Estonia
- France
- Ghana

- Greece
- Guatemala
- Iceland
- Ireland
- Italy
- Lesotho
- Malta
- Nambia
- New Zealand
- Finland
- Panama
- Poland
- Russia
- St. Lucia
- Slovenia
- Sri Lanka
- Turkey
- Uruguay

- Grenada
- Hungary
- Iran
- Israel
- Latvia
- Liechtenstein
- Morocco
- Netherlands
- Nigeria
- Pakistan
- Peru
- Portugal
- St. Christopher and Nevis
- Slovak Republic
- South Africa
- Sweden
- Uganda

APPENDIX
B
★ USCIS SERVICE CENTERS ★

California Service Center

U.S. Department of Homeland Security
U.S. Citizenship and Immigration Services
California Service Center
P.O. Box 30111
Laguna Niguel, CA 92607-0111

Texas Service Center

USCIS Texas Service Center
P.O. Box 851488
Mesquite, TX 75185-1488

Vermont Service Center

U.S. Department of Homeland Security
U.S. Citizenship and Immigration Services
Vermont Service Center
75 Lower Welden St.
Saint Albans, VT 05479

Nebraska Service Center

U.S. Department of Homeland Security
U.S. Citizenship and Immigration Services
Nebraska Service Center
850 S. Street
Lincoln, NE   68508

APPENDIX
C
★ IMMIGRATION ACTS ★

IMMIGRATION ACTS

There have been a number of immigration acts in the United States. Some of the most significant ones are listed below:

- The Naturalization Act of 1790 established the rules for naturalized citizenship.

- The Emergency Quota Act of 1921 established national quotas on immigration based on the number of foreign-born residents of each nationality who were living in the United States as of the 1910 census.

- The Immigration Act of 1924 aimed at freezing the current ethnic distribution in response to rising immigration from southern and eastern Europe, as well as Asia.

- The Immigration and Nationality Act of 1952 (or McCarran-Walter Act) liberalized immigration from Asia somewhat, but increased the power of the government to deport illegal immigrants suspected of communist sympathies.

- The Immigration and Nationality Act of 1965 discontinued quotas based on national origin, while giving preference to those who have U.S. relatives. For the first time, Mexican immigration was restricted.

APPENDIX
D
NEW INFORMATION AND
★ PROPOSED LEGISLATION ★

THE CHILD CITIZENSHIP LAW

The Child Citizenship Act of 2000 went into effect on February 27, 2001.

The law has the following effects:

- A child adopted abroad becomes a U.S. citizen immediately upon entry into the United States as a lawful permanent resident.

- A child born abroad to parents, one or both of whom are U.S. citizens, but who is not recognized as a U.S. citizen for various reasons, can also benefit from the new law; i.e., that child becomes a U.S. citizen immediately upon entry into the United States as a lawful permanent resident.

- Subject to its jurisdiction (essentially meaning anyone other than a child of foreign government representatives with diplomatic immunity).

- Indians and other aboriginal people born in the U.S.

- Anyone born outside the U.S., if at least one parent is a U.S. citizen and certain residency or physical presence requirements were fulfilled by the citizen parent or parents prior to the child's birth.

- Anyone who is found in the United States while under five years of age, whose parents cannot be identified, and who is not shown prior to his or her 21st birthday to have been born outside the U.S.

APPENDIX
E
★ USCIS FEE SCHEDULE ★

The following is the USCIS Fee Schedule, effective July 30, 2007. You can also find the full schedule online at **http://www.uscis.gov/files/nativedocuments/FinalUSCISFeeSchedule052907.pdf.**

FORM #	PURPOSE	FEE
I 90	Renew or replace your permanent resident card (green card)	
	If filing to renew your card within 30 days of turning 14	No Fee
	All others where a fee is required: filing + biometric=	$370
I 102	Replace or receive an I-94 Nonimmigrant Arrival-Departure Record	$320
I 129	Petition for nonimmigrant worker	$320
	Note: Petitions for H-1B, H2B, and L-1 workers must also include the supplemental fees and fraud prevention fees described on the form. Those fee amounts are unchanged.	
I 129F	Fiancée petition	
	General fiancée petition	$455
	For K-3 status based on an immigrant petition filed by the same U.S. citizen husband or wife	No fee
I 130	Relative petition	$355

FORM #	PURPOSE	FEE
I 131	Reentry permit, refugee travel document, or advance parole	
	Reentry permit or refugee travel document	$305
	Advanced parole	$305
I 140	Petition for an immigrant worker	$475
I 191	Permission to return to an unrelinquished domicile	$545
I 192	Advance permission to enter as a nonimmigrant	$545
I 193	Waive passport and/or visa requirement to enter the U.S.	$545
I 212	Permission to reapply for admission to the U.S. after deportation or removal	$545
I 290B	Appeal: Motion to reopen or reconsider	$585
I 360	Petition for Amerasian, widow(er) of U.S.C. or Special Immigrant	
	For Amerasian	No fee
	Self-petitioning battered or abused spouse, parent, or child of a U.S. citizen or permanent resident	No fee
	Special Immigrant Juvenile	No fee
	All others	$375
I 485	Adjust status and become a permanent resident while in the U.S.	
	Applying based on your having been admitted to the U.S. as a refugee	No fee
	All other eligibility:	
	If under 14 and: -filing with the I-485 application of at least one parent	$600
	-not filing with the I-485 application of at least one parent	$930
	If 79 or older	$930
	All others: filing + biometric=	$1,010
	Note: The penalty fee, where it applies, is in addition to the above fees, and is unchanged.	

FORM #	PURPOSE	FEE
I 526	Investor petition	$1,435
I 539	Extend stay as nonimmigrant or change nonimmigrant status	$300
I 589	Asylum	No Fee
I 600A	Advance processing for orphan petition Note: If you already have approved I-600A that is about to expire, and have not yet filed your I-600 petition, you can receive one free extension of your I-600A by filing a new I-600A without fee before the first expires.	$750 (filing + biometric) for you + $80 biometric fee for each person 18 or older living with you
I 600	Orphan petition If based on an approved I-600A Otherwise	No fee $750 (filing + biometric) for you + $80 biometric fee for each person 18 or older living with you
I 601	Waive grounds of excludability	$545
I 612	Waive foreign residence requirement	$545
I 730	Refugee/asylee relative petition	No fee
I 751	Remove conditions on your permanent resident status	$545 (filing + biometric) for you + $80 biometric fee for each dependent you include in your application
I 765	Employment Authorization / Employment Authorization Document (EAD)	$340

FORM #	PURPOSE	FEE
I 821	Temporary Protected Status (TPS) Program First-time applicant If under 14 and not applying for EAD Otherwise: filing + biometric = Renewal or reregistration: biometric=	 $50 $130 $80
I 824	Follow-up action on an approved application or petition	$340
I 829	Remove conditions on permanent resident status (investor)	$2,930 (filing + biometric) for you + $80 biometric fee for each dependent you include in your application
I 881	NACARA — suspension of deportation or special rule Filed with USCIS - A base filing fee of $285 per person, with a base fee family cap of $570 for applications filed together by a husband, wife, and unmarried children. Each applicant must also pay an $80 biometric fee. Filed with the Immigration Court	 $165
I 905	Authorization for organization to issue certification to health care workers	$230
I 907	Premium processing fee	$1,000
I 914	For "T" nonimmigrant status	No fee
U.S. CITIZENSHIP		
N 300	To file Declaration of Intent to apply for U.S. Citizenship	$235
N 336	Request hearing on decision on naturalization application	$605
N 400	Naturalization (to become a U.S. citizen) Through service in the U.S. armed forces All others: filing + biometric =	 No fee $675
N 470	Preserve residence for naturalization purposes	$305
N 565	Replace naturalization / citizenship certificate	$380

FORM #	PURPOSE	FEE
N 600	Recognition of U.S. citizenship	
N 600K	For biological child	$460
	for adopted child	$420
N 644	Posthumous citizenship	No fee

PROGRAMS UNDER THE 1986 LEGALIZATION AND SPECIAL AGRICULTURAL WORKER (SAW) PROGRAMS

FORM #	PURPOSE	FEE
I 687	Become a temporary resident: filing + biometric=	$790
I 690	Waive grounds of excludability	$185
I 694	Appeal	$545
I 695	Replace temporary resident card or Employment Authorization Document: filing + biometric=	$210
I 698	Temporary resident's application for permanent resident status:	
	Filed within 31 months after granted temporary residence: Filing + biometric=	$1,450
	Filed later: filing + biometric=	$1,490
I 817	Status under Family Unity Program	
	If under 14	$440
	All others: filing + biometric=	$520

Please be sure you include the correct fee. Cases with the wrong fee will be rejected. Your payment must be in U.S. dollars. Checks and money orders must be from U.S. institutions. Do not mail cash. Checks are accepted subject to collection. Make your check out to "Department of Homeland Security" except that:

- If you are filing an I-881 with the Immigration Court, make your payment out to the "Department of Justice."

- If you live in Guam, make your payment out to "Treasurer, Guam."

- If you live in the U.S. Virgin Islands, make your payment out to "Commissioner of Finance of the Virgin Islands."

Please spell the name out completely. Do not use initials, such as DHS. Filing and biometric fees cannot be refunded. We may use electronic check conversion for the payment process. Our returned check fee is $30.

Fee waivers — USCIS has already waived fees for certain kinds of cases and circumstances. In other instances an applicant or petitioner who believes that they are financially unable to pay that fee even though others must pay that fee can apply for a fee waiver. Waiver requests can only be considered for the following forms: I-90, I-751, I-765, I-817, N-300, N-400, N-470, N-565, N-600, N-600K, the I-485 if adjustment of status if based on asylum status, on "T" or "U" nonimmigrant status, on an approved self-petitioning battered or abused spouse, parent, or child of a U.S. citizen or permanent resident, or to whom the public charge provisions do not apply; and the I-290B and N-336 appeals and motions for the above forms. For more information about how to apply, and how to prove eligibility for a waiver, see our Web site or call us at 1-800-375-5283.

Copies of documents — If you are applying to renew or replace a card or USCIS document, and the instructions say to include your current one when you apply, then you must submit your actual card or document. For all other applications and petitions, you can submit legible photocopies of documents such as a naturalization certificate, birth certificate, marriage certificate, divorce decree, or permanent resident card. Any copy must be a complete copy of the front and back. As we process your case we may ask you for the original for verification.

Adjustment applications and ancillary benefits — The new application fee for an I-485 is a package fee that includes associated EAD and advance parole applications. Thus, if you file an I-485 with the fee listed above, while you will still need to submit applications for an EAD and advance parole, you will not need to pay a separate fee so long as your adjustment application is pending. However, if you filed your I-485 before this fee change, to apply for or renew your EAD or advance parole, you must file a new application with the new fee for those applications.

★ PRESIDENTS ★

1.   George Washington, 1789-1797

2.   John Adams, 1797-1801

3.   Thomas Jefferson, 1801-1809

4.   James Madison, 1809-1817

5.   James Monroe, 1817-1825

6.   John Quincy Adams, 1825-1829

7.   Andrew Jackson, 1829-1837

8.   Martin Van Buren, 1837-1841

9.   William Henry Harrison, 1841

10. John Tyler, 1841-1845

11. James Knox Polk, 1845-1849

12. Zachary Taylor, 1849-1850

13. Millard Fillmore, 1850-1853

14. Franklin Pierce, 1853-1857

15. James Buchanan, 1857-1861

16. Abraham Lincoln, 1861-1865

17. Andrew Johnson, 1865-1869

18. Ulysses Simpson Grant, 1869-1877

19. Rutherford Birchard Hayes, 1877-1881

20. James Abram Garfield, 1881

21. Chester Alan Arthur, 1881-1885

22. Grover Cleveland, 1885-1889

23. Benjamin Harrison, 1889-1893

24. Grover Cleveland, 1893-1897

25. William McKinley, 1897-1901

26. Theodore Roosevelt, 1901-1909

27. William Howard Taft, 1909-1913

28. Woodrow Wilson, 1913-1921

29. Warren Gamaliel Harding, 1921-1923

30. Calvin Coolidge, 1923-1929

31. Herbert Clark Hoover, 1929-1933

32. Franklin Delano Roosevelt, 1933-1945

33. Harry S. Truman, 1945-1953

34. Dwight David Eisenhower, 1953-1961

35. John Fitzgerald Kennedy, 1961-1963

36. Lyndon Baines Johnson, 1963-1969

37. Richard Milhous Nixon, 1969-1974

38. Gerald Rudolph Ford, 1974-1977

39. James Earl Carter, Jr., 1977-1981

40. Ronald Wilson Reagan, 1981-1989

41. George Herbert Walker Bush, 1989-1993

42. William Jefferson Clinton, 1993-2001

43. George Walker Bush, 2001-2009

44. Barack Hussein Obama 2009-

★ AMERICAN FACT: *THE BALD EAGLE* ★

The Bald Eagle is the national bird of the United States of America. It is one of the country's most recognizable symbols, and appears on most of its official seals, including the Seal of the President of the United States. The Continental Congress adopted the current design for the Great Seal of the United States including a Bald Eagle grasping thirteen arrows and a thirteen-leaf olive branch with its talons on June 20, 1782. It can be found on both national seals and on the back of several coins (including the quarter dollar coin until 1999).

Source: http://en.wikipedia.org/wiki/National_bird_of_the_United_States#National_bird_of_the_United_States

APPENDIX
G
★ THE CONSTITUTION ★

The U.S. Constitution, written in 1787, outlines the principles that form the basis for the U.S. government and establishes the basis for a representative democracy. In 1787, a constitutional convention was held at Independence Hall in Philadelphia, Pennsylvania. A new constitution was written, and it was ratified by the states in 1788.

Following is the U.S. Constitution. The Amendments can be found in Appendix H.

PREAMBLE

We the people of the United States, in order to form a more perfect union, establish justice, insure domestic tranquility, provide for the common defense, promote the general welfare, and secure the blessings of liberty to ourselves and our posterity, do ordain and establish this Constitution for the United States of America.

ARTICLE ONE

Section 1. *All legislative powers herein granted shall be vested in a Congress of the United States, which shall consist of a Senate and House of Representatives.*

Section 2. *The House of Representatives shall be composed of members chosen every second year by the people of the several states, and the electors in each state shall have the qualifications requisite for electors of the most numerous branch of the state legislature.*

No person shall be a Representative who shall not have attained to the age of twenty five years, and been seven years a citizen of the United States, and who shall not, when elected, be an inhabitant of that state in which he shall be chosen.

Representatives and direct taxes shall be apportioned among the several states which may be included within this union, according to their respective numbers, which shall be determined by adding to the whole number of free persons, including those bound to service for a term of years, and excluding Indians not taxed, three fifths of all other Persons. The actual Enumeration shall be made within three years after the first meeting of the Congress of the United States, and within every subsequent term of ten years, in such manner as they shall by law direct. The number of Representatives shall not exceed one for every thirty thousand, but each state shall have at least one Representative; and until such enumeration shall be made, the state of New Hampshire shall be entitled to choose three, Massachusetts eight, Rhode Island and Providence Plantations one, Connecticut five, New York six, New Jersey four, Pennsylvania eight, Delaware one, Maryland six, Virginia ten, North Carolina five, South Carolina five, and Georgia three.

When vacancies happen in the Representation from any state, the executive authority thereof shall issue writs of election to fill such vacancies.

The House of Representatives shall choose their speaker and other officers; and shall have the sole power of impeachment.

Section 3. *The Senate of the United States shall be composed of two Senators from each state, chosen by the legislature thereof, for six years; and each Senator shall have one vote.*

Immediately after they shall be assembled in consequence of the first election, they shall be divided as equally as may be into three classes. The seats of the Senators of the first class shall be vacated at the expiration of the second year, of the second class at the expiration of the fourth year, and the third class at the expiration of the sixth year, so that one third may be chosen every second year; and if vacancies happen by resignation, or otherwise, during the recess of the legislature of any state, the executive thereof may make temporary appointments until the next meeting of the legislature, which shall then fill such vacancies.

No person shall be a Senator who shall not have attained to the age of thirty years, and been nine years a citizen of the United States and who shall not, when elected, be an inhabitant of that state for which he shall be chosen.

The Vice President of the United States shall be President of the Senate, but shall have no vote, unless they be equally divided.

The Senate shall choose their other officers, and also a President pro tempore, in the absence of the Vice President, or when he shall exercise the office of President of the United States.

The Senate shall have the sole power to try all impeachments. When sitting for that purpose, they shall be on oath or affirmation. When the President of the United States is tried, the Chief Justice shall preside: And no person shall be convicted without the concurrence of two thirds of the members present.

Judgment in cases of impeachment shall not extend further than to removal from office, and disqualification to hold and enjoy any office of honor, trust or profit under the United States: but the party convicted shall nevertheless be liable and subject to indictment, trial, judgment and punishment, according to law.

Section 4. The times, places and manner of holding elections for Senators and Representatives, shall be prescribed in each state by the legislature thereof; but the Congress may at any time by law make or alter such regulations, except as to the places of choosing Senators.

The Congress shall assemble at least once in every year, and such meeting shall be on the first Monday in December, unless they shall by law appoint a different day.

Section 5. Each House shall be the judge of the elections, *returns and qualifications of its own members, and a majority of each shall constitute a quorum to do business; but a smaller number may adjourn from day to day, and may be authorized to compel the attendance of absent members, in such manner, and under such penalties as each House may provide.*

Each House may determine the rules of its proceedings, punish its members for disorderly behavior, and, with the concurrence of two thirds, expel a member.

Each House shall keep a journal of its proceedings, and from time to time publish the same, excepting such parts as may in their judgment require secrecy; and the yeas and nays of the members of either House on any question shall, at the desire of one fifth of those present, be entered on the journal.

Neither House, during the session of Congress, shall, without the consent of the other, adjourn for more than three days, nor to any other place than that in which the two Houses shall be sitting.

Section 6. *The Senators and Representatives shall receive a compensation for their services, to be ascertained by law, and paid out of the treasury of the United States. They shall in all cases, except treason, felony and breach of the peace, be privileged from arrest during their attendance at the session of their respective Houses, and in going to and returning from the same; and for any speech or debate in either House, they shall not be questioned in any other place.*

No Senator or Representative shall, during the time for which he was elected, be appointed to any civil office under the authority of the United States, which shall have been created, or the emoluments whereof shall have been increased during such time: and no person holding any office under the United States, shall be a member of either House during his continuance in office.

Section 7. *All bills for raising revenue shall originate in the House of Representatives; but the Senate may propose or concur with amendments as on other bills.*

Every bill which shall have passed the House of Representatives and the Senate, shall, before it become a law, be presented to the President of the United States; if he approve he shall sign it, but if not he shall return it, with his objections to that House in which it shall have originated, who shall enter the objections at large on their journal, and proceed to reconsider it. If after such reconsideration two thirds of that House shall agree to pass the bill, it shall be sent, together with the objections, to the other House, by which it shall likewise be reconsidered, and if approved by two thirds of that House, it shall become a law. But in all such cases the votes of both Houses shall be determined by yeas and nays, and the names of the persons voting for and against the bill shall be entered on the journal of each House respectively. If any bill shall not be returned by the President within ten days (Sundays excepted) after it shall have been presented to him, the same shall be a law, in like manner as if he had signed it, unless the Congress by their adjournment prevent its return, in which case it shall not be a law.

Every order, resolution, or vote to which the concurrence of the Senate and House of Representatives may be necessary (except on a question of adjournment) shall be presented to the President of the United States; and before the same shall take effect, shall be approved by him, or being disapproved by him, shall be repassed by two thirds of the Senate and House of Representatives, according to the rules and limitations prescribed in the case of a bill.

Section 8. *The Congress shall have power to lay and collect taxes, duties, imposts and excises, to pay the debts and provide for the common defense and general welfare of the United States; but all duties, imposts and excises shall be uniform throughout the United States;*

To borrow money on the credit of the United States;

To regulate commerce with foreign nations, and among the several states, and with the Indian tribes;

To establish a uniform rule of naturalization, and uniform laws on the subject of bankruptcies throughout the United States;

To coin money, regulate the value thereof, and of foreign coin, and fix the standard of weights and measures;

To provide for the punishment of counterfeiting the securities and current coin of the United States;

To establish post offices and post roads;

To promote the progress of science and useful arts, by securing for limited times to authors and inventors the exclusive right to their respective writings and discoveries;

To constitute tribunals inferior to the Supreme Court;

To define and punish piracies and felonies committed on the high seas, and offenses against the law of nations;

To declare war, grant letters of marque and reprisal, and make rules concerning captures on land and water;

To raise and support armies, but no appropriation of money to that use shall be for a longer term than two years;

To provide and maintain a navy;

To make rules for the government and regulation of the land and naval forces;

To provide for calling forth the militia to execute the laws of the union, suppress insurrections and repel invasions;

To provide for organizing, arming, and disciplining, the militia, and for governing such part of them as may be employed in the service of the United States, reserving to the states respectively, the appointment of the officers, and the authority of training the militia according to the discipline prescribed by Congress;

To exercise exclusive legislation in all cases whatsoever, over such District (not exceeding ten miles square) as may, by cession of particular states, and the acceptance of Congress, become the seat of the government of the United States, and to exercise like authority over all places purchased by the consent of the legislature of the state in which the same shall be, for the erection of forts, magazines, arsenals, dockyards, and other needful buildings; —And,

To make all laws which shall be necessary and proper for carrying into execution the foregoing powers, and all other powers vested by this Constitution in the government of the United States, or in any department or officer thereof.

Section 9. *The migration or importation of such persons as any of the states now existing shall think proper to admit, shall not be prohibited by the Congress prior to the year one thousand eight hundred and eight, but a tax or duty may be imposed on such importation, not exceeding ten dollars for each person.*

The privilege of the writ of habeas corpus shall not be suspended, unless when in cases of rebellion or invasion the public safety may require it.

No bill of attainder or ex post facto law shall be passed.

No capitation, or other direct, tax shall be laid, unless in proportion to the census or enumeration herein before directed to be taken.

No tax or duty shall be laid on articles exported from any state.

No preference shall be given by any regulation of commerce or revenue to the ports of one state over those of another: nor shall vessels bound to, or from, one state, be obliged to enter, clear or pay duties in another.

No money shall be drawn from the treasury, but in consequence of appropriations made by law; and a regular statement and account of receipts and expenditures of all public money shall be published from time to time.

No title of nobility shall be granted by the United States: and no person holding any office of profit or trust under them, shall, without the consent of the Congress, accept of any present, emolument, office, or title, of any kind whatever, from any king, prince, or foreign state.

Section 10. *No state shall enter into any treaty, alliance, or confederation; grant letters of marque and reprisal; coin money; emit bills of credit; make anything but gold and silver coin a tender in payment of debts; pass any bill of attainder, ex post facto law, or law impairing the obligation of contracts, or grant any title of nobility.*

No state shall, without the consent of the Congress, lay any imposts or duties on imports or exports, except what may be absolutely necessary for executing its inspection laws: and the net produce of all duties and imposts, laid by any state on imports or exports, shall be for the use of the treasury of the United States; and all such laws shall be subject to the revision and control of the Congress.

No state shall, without the consent of Congress, lay any duty of tonnage, keep troops, or ships of war in time of peace, enter into any agreement or compact with another state, or with a foreign power, or engage in war, unless actually invaded, or in such imminent danger as will not admit of delay.

ARTICLE TWO

Section 1. *The executive power shall be vested in a President of the United States of America. He shall hold his office during the term of four years, and, together with the Vice President, chosen for the same term, be elected, as follows:*

Each state shall appoint, in such manner as the Legislature thereof may direct, a number of electors, equal to the whole number of Senators and Representatives to which the State may be entitled in the Congress: but no Senator or Representative, or person holding an office of trust or profit under the United States, shall be appointed an elector.

The electors shall meet in their respective states, and vote by ballot for two persons, of whom one at least shall not be an inhabitant of the same state with themselves. And they shall make a list of all the persons voted for, and of the number of votes for each; which list they shall sign and certify, and transmit sealed to the seat of the government of the United States, directed to the President of the Senate. The President *of the Senate shall, in the presence of the Senate and House of Representatives, open all the certificates, and the votes shall then be counted. The person having the greatest number of votes shall be the President, if such number be a majority of the whole number of electors appointed; and if there be more than one who have such majority, and have an equal number of votes, then the House of Representatives shall immediately choose by ballot one of them for President; and if no person have a majority, then from the five highest on the list the said House shall in like manner choose the President. But in choosing the President, the votes shall be taken by states, the representation from each state having one vote; a quorum for this purpose shall consist of a member or members from two thirds of the states, and a majority of all the states shall be necessary to a choice. In every case, after the choice of the President, the person having the greatest number of votes of the electors shall be the Vice President. But if there should remain two or more who have equal votes, the Senate shall choose from them by ballot the Vice President.*

The Congress may determine the time of choosing the electors, and the day on which they shall give their votes; which day shall be the same throughout the United States.

No person except a natural born citizen, or a citizen of the United States, at the time of the adoption of this Constitution, shall be eligible to the office of President; neither shall any person be eligible to that office who shall not have attained to the age of thirty-five years, and been fourteen years a resident within the United States.

In case of the removal of the President from office, or of his death, resignation, or inability to discharge the powers and duties of the said office, the same shall devolve on the Vice President, and the Congress may by law provide for the case of removal, death, resignation or inability, both of the President and Vice President, declaring what officer shall then act as President, and such officer shall act accordingly, until the disability be removed, or a President shall be elected.

The President shall, at stated times, receive for his services, a compensation, which shall neither be increased nor diminished during the period for which he shall have been elected, and he shall not receive within that period any other emolument from the United States, or any of them.

Before he enter on the execution of his office, he shall take the following oath or affirmation: "I do solemnly swear (or affirm) that I will faithfully execute the office of President of the United States, and will to the best of my ability preserve, protect and defend the Constitution of the United States."

Section 2. The President shall be commander in chief of the Army and Navy of the United States, and of the militia of the several states, when called into the actual service of the United States; he may require the opinion, in writing, of the principal officer in each of the executive departments, upon any subject relating to the duties of their respective offices, and he shall have power to grant reprieves and pardons for offenses against the United States, except in cases of impeachment.

He shall have power, by and with the advice and consent of the Senate, to make treaties, provided two thirds of the Senators present concur; and he shall nominate, and by and with the advice and consent of the Senate, shall appoint ambassadors, other public ministers and consuls, judges of the Supreme Court, and all other officers of the United States, whose appointments are not herein otherwise provided for, and which shall be established by law: but the Congress may by law vest the appointment of such inferior officers, as *they think proper, in the President alone, in the courts of law, or in the heads of departments.*

The President shall have power to fill up all vacancies that may happen during the recess of the Senate, by granting commissions which shall expire at the end of their next session.

Section 3. *He shall from time to time give to the Congress information of the state of the Union, and recommend to their consideration such measures as he shall judge necessary and expedient; he may, on extraordinary occasions, convene both Houses, or either of them, and in case of disagreement between them, with respect to the time of adjournment, he may adjourn them to such time as he shall think proper; he shall receive ambassadors and other public ministers; he shall take care that the laws be faithfully executed, and shall commission all the officers of the United States.*

Section 4. *The President, Vice President and all civil officers of the United States, shall be removed from office on impeachment for, and conviction of, treason, bribery, or other high crimes and misdemeanors.*

ARTICLE THREE

Section 1. *The judicial power of the United States, shall be vested in one Supreme Court, and in such inferior courts as the Congress may from time to time ordain and establish. The judges, both of the supreme and inferior courts, shall hold their offices during good behavior, and shall, at stated times, receive for their services a compensation, which shall not be diminished during their continuance in office.*

Section 2. *The judicial power shall extend to all cases, in* *law and equity, arising under this Constitution, the laws of the United States, and treaties made, or which shall be made, under their authority; to all cases affecting ambassadors, other public ministers and consuls; to all cases of admiralty and maritime jurisdiction; to controversies to which the United States shall be a party; to controversies between two or more states; between a state and citizens of another state; between citizens of different states; between citizens of the same state claiming lands under grants of different states, and between a state, or the citizens thereof, and foreign states, citizens or subjects.*

In all cases affecting ambassadors, other public ministers and consuls, and those in which a state shall be party, the Supreme Court shall have original jurisdiction. In all the other cases before mentioned, the Supreme Court shall have appellate jurisdiction, both as to law and fact, with such exceptions, and under such regulations as the Congress shall make.

The trial of all crimes, except in cases of impeachment, shall be by jury; and such trial shall be held in the state where the said crimes shall have been committed; but when not committed within any state, the trial shall be at such place or places as the Congress may by law have directed.

Section 3. *Treason against the United States, shall consist only in levying war against them, or in adhering to their enemies, giving them aid and comfort. No person shall be convicted of treason unless on the testimony of two witnesses to the same overt act, or on confession in open court.*

The Congress shall have power to declare the punishment of treason, but no attainder of treason shall work corruption of blood, or forfeiture except during the life of the person attainted.

ARTICLE FOUR

Section 1. *Full faith and credit shall be given in each state to the public acts, records, and judicial proceedings of every other state. And the Congress may by general laws prescribe the manner in which such acts, records, and proceedings shall be proved, and the effect thereof.*

Section 2. *The citizens of each state shall be entitled to all privileges and immunities of citizens in the several states.*

A person charged in any state with treason, felony, or other crime, who shall flee from justice, and be found in another state, shall on demand of the executive authority of the state from which he fled, be delivered up, to be removed to the state having jurisdiction of the crime.

No person held to service or labor in one state, under the laws thereof, escaping into another, shall, in consequence of any law or regulation therein, be discharged from such service or labor, but shall be delivered up on claim of the party to whom such service or labor may be due.

Section 3. *New states may be admitted by the Congress into this union; but no new states shall be formed or erected within the jurisdiction of any other state; nor any state be formed by the junction of two or more states, or parts of states, without the consent of the legislatures of the states concerned as well as of the Congress.*

The Congress shall have power to dispose of and make all needful rules and regulations respecting the territory or other property belonging to the United States; and nothing in this Constitution shall be so construed as to prejudice any claims of the United States, or of any particular state.

Section 4. The United States shall guarantee to every state in this union a republican form of government, and shall protect each of them against invasion; and on application of the legislature, or of the executive (when the legislature cannot be convened) against domestic violence.

ARTICLE FIVE

The Congress, whenever two thirds of both houses shall deem it necessary, shall propose amendments to this Constitution, or, on the application of the legislatures of two thirds of the several states, shall call a convention for proposing amendments, which, in either case, shall be valid to all intents and purposes, as part of this Constitution, when ratified by the legislatures of three fourths of the several states, or by conventions in three fourths thereof, as the one or the other mode of ratification may be proposed by the Congress; provided that no amendment which may be made prior to the year one thousand eight hundred and eight shall in any manner affect the first and fourth clauses in the ninth section of the first article; and that no state, without its consent, shall be deprived of its equal suffrage in the Senate.

ARTICLE SIX

All debts contracted and engagements entered into, before the adoption of this Constitution, shall be as valid against the United States under this Constitution, as under the Confederation.

This Constitution, and the laws of the United States which shall be made in pursuance thereof; and all treaties made, or which shall be made, under the authority of the United States, shall be the supreme law of the land; and the judges in every state shall be bound thereby, anything in the Constitution or laws of any State to the contrary notwithstanding.

The Senators and Representatives before mentioned, and the members of the several state legislatures, and all executive and judicial officers, both of the United States and of the several states, shall be bound by oath or affirmation, to support this Constitution; but no religious test shall ever be required as a qualification to any office or public trust under the United States.

ARTICLE SEVEN

The ratification of the conventions of nine states, shall be sufficient for the establishment of this Constitution between the states so ratifying the same.

THE SIGNERS

Done in convention by the unanimous consent of the states present the seventeenth day of September in the year of our Lord one thousand seven hundred and eighty-seven and of the independence of the United States of America the twelfth.

In witness whereof We have hereunto subscribed our Names,

G. Washington-President and deputy from Virginia

New Hampshire: John Langdon, Nicholas Gilman

Massachusetts: Nathaniel Gorham, Rufus King

Connecticut: Wm: Saml. Johnson, Roger Sherman

New York: Alexander Hamilton

New Jersey: Wil. Livingston, David Brearly, Wm. Paterson, Jona. Dayton

Pennsylvania: B. Franklin, Thomas Mifflin, Robt. Morris, Geo. Clymer, Thos. FitzSimons, Jared Ingersoll, James Wilson, Gouv Morris

Delaware: Geo. Read, Gunning Bedford jun, John Dickinson, Richard Bassett, Jaco. Broom

Maryland: James McHenry, Dan of St Thos. Jenifer, Danl Carroll

Virginia: John Blair, James Madison Jr.

North Carolina: Wm. Blount, Richd. Dobbs Spaight, Hu Williamson

South Carolina: J. Rutledge, Charles Cotesworth Pinckney, Charles Pinckney, Pierce Butler

Georgia: William Few, Abr Baldwin

APPENDIX
H
★ THE AMENDMENTS ★

Following are the amendments to the constitution.

AMENDMENT I

Congress shall make no law respecting an establishment of religion, or prohibiting the free exercise thereof; or abridging the freedom of speech, or of the press; or the right of the people peaceably to assemble, and to petition the government for a redress of grievances.

AMENDMENT II

A well regulated militia, being necessary to the security of a free state, the right of the people to keep and bear arms, shall not be infringed.

AMENDMENT III

No soldier shall, in time of peace be quartered in any house, without the consent of the owner, nor in time of war, but in a manner to be prescribed by law.

AMENDMENT **IV**

The right of the people to be secure in their persons, houses, papers, and effects, against unreasonable searches and seizures, shall not be violated, and no warrants shall issue, but upon probable cause, supported by oath or affirmation, and particularly describing the place to be searched, and the persons or things to be seized.

AMENDMENT **V**

No person shall be held to answer for a capital, or otherwise infamous crime, unless on a presentment or indictment of a grand jury, except in cases arising in the land or naval forces, or in the militia, when in actual service in time of war or public danger; nor shall any person be subject for the same offense to be twice put in jeopardy of life or limb; nor shall be compelled in any criminal case to be a witness against himself, nor be deprived of life, liberty, or property, without due process of law; nor shall private property be taken for public use, without just compensation.

AMENDMENT **VI**

In all criminal prosecutions, the accused shall enjoy the right to a speedy and public trial, by an impartial jury of the state and district wherein the crime shall have been committed, which district shall have been previously ascertained by law, and to be informed of the nature and cause of the accusation; to be confronted with the witnesses against him; to have compulsory process for obtaining witnesses in his favor, and to have the assistance of counsel for his defense.

AMENDMENT VII

In suits at common law, where the value in controversy shall exceed twenty dollars, the right of trial by jury shall be preserved, and no fact tried by a jury, shall be otherwise reexamined in any court of the United States, than according to the rules of the common law.

AMENDMENT VIII

Excessive bail shall not be required, nor excessive fines imposed, nor cruel and unusual punishments inflicted.

AMENDMENT IX

The enumeration in the Constitution, of certain rights, shall not be construed to deny or disparage others retained by the people.

AMENDMENT X

The powers not delegated to the United States by the Constitution, nor prohibited by it to the states, are reserved to the states respectively, or to the people.

AMENDMENT XI

The judicial power of the United States shall not be construed to extend to any suit in law or equity, commenced or prosecuted against one of the United States by citizens of another state, or by citizens or subjects of any foreign state.

AMENDMENT XII

The electors shall meet in their respective states and vote by ballot for President and Vice-President, one of whom, at least, shall not be an inhabitant of the same state with themselves; they shall name in their ballots the person voted for as President, and in distinct ballots the person voted for as Vice-President, and they shall make distinct lists of all persons voted for as President, and of all persons voted for as Vice-President, and of the number of votes for each, which lists they shall sign and certify, and transmit sealed to the seat of the government of the United States, directed to the President of the Senate. The President of the Senate shall, in the presence of the Senate and House of Representatives, open all the certificates and the votes shall then be counted; the person having the greatest number of votes for President, shall be the President, if such number be a majority of the whole number of electors appointed; and if no person have such majority, then from the persons having the highest numbers not exceeding three on the list of those voted for as President, the House of Representatives shall choose immediately, by ballot, the President. But in choosing the President, the votes shall be taken by states, the representation from each state having one vote; a quorum for this purpose shall consist of a member or members from two-thirds of the states, and a majority of all the states shall be necessary to a choice. And if the House of Representatives shall not choose a President whenever the right of choice shall devolve upon them, before the fourth day of March next following, then the Vice-President shall act as President, as in the case of the death or other constitutional disability of the President. The person having the greatest number of votes as Vice-President, shall be the Vice-President, if such number be a majority of the whole number of electors appointed, and if no person have a majority, then from the two highest numbers on the list, the Senate shall choose the Vice-President; a quorum for the purpose shall consist of two-thirds of the whole number of Senators, and a majority of the whole number shall be necessary to a choice. But no person constitutionally ineligible to the office of President shall be eligible to that of Vice-President of the United States.

AMENDMENT XIII

Section 1. Neither slavery nor involuntary servitude, except as a punishment for crime whereof the party shall have been duly convicted, shall exist within the United States, or any place subject to their jurisdiction.

Section 2. Congress shall have power to enforce this article by appropriate legislation.

AMENDMENT XIV

Section 1. All persons born or naturalized in the United States, and subject to the jurisdiction thereof, are citizens of the United States and of the state wherein they reside. No state shall make or enforce any law which shall abridge the privileges or immunities of citizens of the United States; nor shall any state deprive any person of life, liberty, or property, without due process of law; nor deny to any person within its jurisdiction the equal protection of the laws.

Section 2. Representatives shall be apportioned among the several states according to their respective numbers, counting the whole number of persons in each state, excluding Indians not taxed. But when the right to vote at any election for the choice of electors for President and Vice President of the United States, Representatives in Congress, the executive and judicial officers of a state, or the members of the legislature thereof, is denied to any of the male inhabitants of such state, being twenty-one years of age, and citizens of the United States, or in any way abridged, except for participation in rebellion, or other crime, the basis of representation therein shall be reduced in the proportion which the number of such male citizens shall bear to the whole number of male citizens twenty-one years of age in such state.

Section 3. No person shall be a Senator or Representative in Congress, or elector of President and Vice President, or hold any office, civil or military, under the United States, or under any state, who, having previously taken an oath, as a member of Congress, or as an officer of the United States, or as a member of any state legislature, or as an executive or judicial officer of any state, to support the Constitution of the United States, shall have engaged in insurrection or rebellion against the same, or given aid or comfort to the enemies thereof. But Congress may by a vote of two-thirds of each House, remove such disability.

Section 4. The validity of the public debt of the United States, authorized by law, including debts incurred for payment of pensions and bounties for services in suppressing insurrection or rebellion, shall not be questioned. But neither the United States nor any state shall assume or pay any debt or obligation incurred in aid of insurrection or rebellion against the United States, or any claim for the loss or emancipation of any slave; but all such debts, obligations and claims shall be held illegal and void.

Section 5. The Congress shall have power to enforce, by appropriate legislation, the provisions of this article.

AMENDMENT XV

Section 1. The right of citizens of the United States to vote shall not be denied or abridged by the United States or by any state on account of race, color, or previous condition of servitude.

Section 2. The Congress shall have power to enforce this article by appropriate legislation.

AMENDMENT XVI

The Congress shall have power to lay and collect taxes on incomes, from whatever source derived, without apportionment among the several states, and without regard to any census or enumeration.

AMENDMENT XVII

The Senate of the United States shall be composed of two Senators from each state, elected by the people thereof, for six years; and each Senator shall have one vote. The electors in each state shall have the qualifications requisite for electors of the most numerous branch of the state legislatures.

When vacancies happen in the representation of any state in the Senate, the executive authority of each state shall issue writs of election to fill such vacancies: Provided, that the legislature of any state may empower the executive thereof to make temporary appointments until the people fill the vacancies by election as the legislature may direct.

This amendment shall not be so construed as to affect the election or term of any Senator chosen before it becomes valid as part of the Constitution.

Amendment XVIII

Section 1. *After one year from the ratification of this article the manufacture, sale, or transportation of intoxicating liquors within, the importation thereof into, or the exportation thereof from the United States and all territory subject to the jurisdiction thereof for beverage purposes is hereby prohibited.*

Section 2. *The Congress and the several states shall have concurrent power to enforce this article by appropriate legislation.*

Section 3. *This article shall be inoperative unless it shall have been ratified as an amendment to the Constitution by the legislatures of the several states, as provided in the Constitution, within seven years from the date of the submission hereof to the states by the Congress.*

Amendment XIX

The right of citizens of the United States to vote shall not be denied or abridged by the United States or by any state on account of sex.

Congress shall have power to enforce this article by appropriate legislation.

Amendment XX

Section 1. *The terms of the President and Vice President shall end at noon on the 20th day of January, and the terms of Senators and Representatives at noon on the 3d day of January, of the years in which such terms would have ended if this article had not been ratified; and the terms of their successors shall then begin.*

Section 2. The Congress shall assemble at least once in every year, and such meeting shall begin at noon on the 3d day of January, unless they shall by law appoint a different day.

Section 3. If, at the time fixed for the beginning of the term of the President, the President elect shall have died, the Vice President elect shall become President. If a President shall not have been chosen before the time fixed for the beginning of his term, or if the President elect shall have failed to qualify, then the Vice President elect shall act as President until a President shall have qualified; and the Congress may by law provide for the case wherein neither a President elect nor a Vice President elect shall have qualified, declaring who shall then act as President, or the manner in which one who is to act shall be selected, and such person shall act accordingly until a President or Vice President shall have qualified.

Section 4. The Congress may by law provide for the case of the death of any of the persons from whom the House of Representatives may choose a President whenever the right of choice shall have devolved upon them, and for the case of the death of any of the persons from whom the Senate may choose a Vice President whenever the right of choice shall have devolved upon them.

Section 5. Sections 1 and 2 shall take effect on the 15th day of October following the ratification of this article.

Section 6. This article shall be inoperative unless it shall have been ratified as an amendment to the Constitution by the legislatures of three-fourths of the several states within seven years from the date of its submission.

AMENDMENT **XXI**

Section 1. The eighteenth article of amendment to the Constitution of the United States is hereby repealed.

Section 2. The transportation or importation into any state, territory, or possession of the United States for delivery or use therein of intoxicating liquors, in violation of the laws thereof, is hereby prohibited.

Section 3. This article shall be inoperative unless it shall have been ratified as an amendment to the Constitution by conventions in the several states, as provided in the Constitution, within seven years from the date of the submission hereof to the states by the Congress.

AMENDMENT **XXII**

Section 1. No person shall be elected to the office of the President more than twice, and no person who has held the office of President, or acted as President, for more than two years of a term to which some other person was elected President shall be elected to the office of the President more than once. But this article shall not apply to any person holding the office of President when this article was proposed by the Congress, and shall not prevent any person who may be holding the office of President, or acting as President, during the term within which this article becomes operative from holding the office of President or acting as President during the remainder of such term.

Section 2. This article shall be inoperative unless it shall have been ratified as an amendment to the Constitution by the legislatures of three-fourths of the several states within seven years from the date of its submission to the states by the Congress.

AMENDMENT **XXIII**

Section 1. *The District constituting the seat of government of the United States shall appoint in such manner as the Congress may direct:*

A number of electors of President and Vice President equal to the whole number of Senators and Representatives in Congress to which the District would be entitled if it were a state, but in no event more than the least populous state; they shall be in addition to those appointed by the states, but they shall be considered, for the purposes of the election of President and Vice President, to be electors appointed by a state; and they shall meet in the District and perform such duties as provided by the twelfth article of amendment.

Section 2. *The Congress shall have power to enforce this article by appropriate legislation.*

AMENDMENT **XXIV**

Section 1. *The right of citizens of the United States to vote in any primary or other election for President or Vice President, for electors for President or Vice President, or for Senator or Representative in Congress, shall not be denied or abridged by the United States or any state by reason of failure to pay any poll tax or other tax.*

Section 2. *The Congress shall have power to enforce this article by appropriate legislation.*

AMENDMENT **XXV**

Section 1. *In case of the removal of the President from office or of his death or resignation, the Vice President shall become President.*

239

Section 2. *Whenever there is a vacancy in the office of the Vice President, the President shall nominate a Vice President who shall take office upon confirmation by a majority vote of both Houses of Congress.*

Section 3. *Whenever the President transmits to the President pro tempore of the Senate and the Speaker of the House of Representatives his written declaration that he is unable to discharge the powers and duties of his office, and until he transmits to them a written declaration to the contrary, such powers and duties shall be discharged by the Vice President as Acting President.*

Section 4. *Whenever the Vice President and a majority of either the principal officers of the executive departments or of such other body as Congress may by law provide, transmit to the President pro tempore of the Senate and the Speaker of the House of Representatives their written declaration that the President is unable to discharge the powers and duties of his office, the Vice President shall immediately assume the powers and duties of the office as Acting President.*

Thereafter, when the President transmits to the President pro tempore of the Senate and the Speaker of the House of Representatives his written declaration that no inability exists, he shall resume the powers and duties of his office unless the Vice President and a majority of either the principal officers of the executive department or of such other body as Congress may by law provide, transmit within four days to the President pro tempore of the Senate and the Speaker of the House of Representatives their written declaration that the President is unable to discharge the powers and duties of his office. Thereupon Congress shall decide the issue, assembling within forty-eight hours for that purpose if not in session. If the Congress, within twenty-one days after receipt of the latter written declaration, or, if Congress is not in session, within twenty-one days after Congress is required to assemble, determines by two-thirds vote of both Houses that the President is unable to discharge the powers and duties of his office, the Vice President shall continue to discharge the same as Acting President; otherwise, the President shall resume the powers and duties of his office.

AMENDMENT **XXVI**

Section 1. The right of citizens of the United States, who are 18 years of age or older, to vote, shall not be denied or abridged by the United States or any state on account of age.

Section 2. The Congress shall have the power to enforce this article by appropriate legislation.

AMENDMENT **XXVII**

No law, varying the compensation for the services of the Senators and Representatives, shall take effect, until an election of Representatives shall have intervened.

★ AMERICAN FACT: *THE MAYFLOWER* ★

The Mayflower was the famous ship that transported the English Separatists, better known as the Pilgrims, from Southampton, England, to Plymouth, Massachusetts in 1620. The vessel left England on September 6 and after a gruelling 66-day journey marked by disease, the ship dropped anchor inside the hook tip of Cape Cod on November 11. The Mayflower originally was destined for the mouth of the Hudson River, near present-day New York City, at the northern edge of England's Virginia colony, which itself was established with the 1607 Jamestown Settlement. However, the Mayflower went off course as the winter approached, and remained in Cape Cod Bay. On March 21, 1621, all surviving passengers, who had inhabited the ship during the winter, moved ashore at Plymouth, and on April 5, the Mayflower, a privately commissioned vessel, returned to England.

Source: http://en.wikipedia.org/wiki/Mayflower

APPENDIX
I
★ TEST ANSWERS ★

1. What holiday was celebrated for the first time by the American colonists?
   D. Thanksgiving

2. Who makes the federal laws in the United States?
   C. Congress

3. What is the Constitution?
   B. The supreme law of the land

4. What is the highest part of the Judiciary Branch of our government?
   B. The Supreme Court

5. A bill becomes law when the President:
   C. Signs it

6. The Pilgrims came to the United States from which of the following countries?
   A. England

7. He was a leader of the Civil Rights Movement:
   C. Martin Luther King

8. The Bill of Rights contains which of the following?
   A. The first 10 amendments

9. When a change is made to the Constitution, it is called:
   C. An amendment

10. The Nineteenth Amendment gave women the right to:
    D. Vote in an election

11. The leader of the Continental Army was:
    B. George Washington

12. The war that occurred between the states is called:
    A. The Civil War

13. The first U.S. capital was in which city?
    C. Philadelphia

14. Which of the following has the power to declare war?
    C. Congress

15. When the President enters into an agreement with a foreign nation that does not require the consent of the Senate it is called:
    B. An executive order

16. How many members are there in the House of Representatives?
    C. 435

17. What do the stripes on the flag represent?
    A. The 13 original states

18. What is the street address of the White House?
    A. 1600 Pennsylvania Avenue

19. Who was the only U.S. President to resign from office?
    D. Richard Nixon

20. The system of checks and balances incorporated into the Constitution ensures that each branch of government has the ability to:
    A. Oversee the powers and actions of the other branches

21. What are the duties of the Supreme Court?
    D. To interpret and explain the laws

22 How many members are there in the Senate?
    C. 100

23. Which part of the government was created to respond most directly to the will of the people?
    B. House of Representatives

24. Who wrote "The Star-Spangled Banner"?
    A. Francis Scott Key

25. What is the term length for a U.S. senator?
    C. 6 years

26. The U.S. gained independence from which country?
C. England

27. Whose rights are guaranteed by the Constitution and the Bill of Rights?
A. All people living in the United States

28. Which of the following is secured by the Bill of Rights?
D. All of the above

29. Who is the current chief justice of the United States?
C. John Roberts, Jr.

30. Who said "Give me liberty or give me death"?
A. Patrick Henry

31. The Great Compromise provided for a (an):
B. Bicameral legislature

32. Which of the following is not a branch of government?
D. The administrative branch

33. According to the U.S. Constitution, a candidate for President must be:
C. Both A and B

34. Who elects the President of the United States?
D. The Electoral College

35. What do the stars on the U.S. flag represent?
A. One for each state

36. *How many changes have there been to the U.S. Constitution?*
B. 27

37. *How long is the term for a member of the House of Representatives?*
A. 2 years

38. *One of the President's checks on judicial power is:*
C. The pardon

39. *Martin Luther King, Jr. urged his people to employ which of the following tactics to achieve justice?*
B. Using peaceful protests to bring about political change

40. *Independence Day in the U.S. is celebrated on which day?*
C. July 4

41. *When a court case is not a criminal violation, it is called:*
A. A civil case

42. *Who was the 43rd President of the United States?*
D. George W. Bush

43. *Which freedom is not protected by the First Amendment?*
D. Freedom to possess firearms

44. Who becomes the President of the United States if the current President dies?
B. The Vice President

45. Who assassinated President John F. Kennedy?
C. Lee Harvey Oswald

46. The disastrous invasion of Cuba in April 1961 became known as the:
C. Bay of Pigs

47. The first official U.S. government could be described as a:
A. Confederation

48. How many terms can the President of the U.S. serve?
B. 2

49. In which city is the Liberty Bell located?
C. Philadelphia

50. Which of the following U.S. Presidents gave the Gettysburg Address?
D. Abraham Lincoln

51. Which of the following states was not a member of the 13 original colonies?
B. Vermont

52. How many states are there in the U.S.?
B. 50

53. *Thomas Jefferson wrote which pair of documents?*
    D. The Northwest Ordinance and the Declaration of Independence

54. *What is the head executive of a state called?*
    A. Governor

55. *Which was the last state to be admitted to the Union?*
    A. Hawaii

56. *The United States currently has two major political parties. Which of the following is one of them?*
    A. Republican

57. *What comprises the legislative branch of the government?*
    B. The Senate and the House of Representatives

58. *What is the Supreme Law of the United States?*
    B. The Constitution

59. *Where does the President of the U.S. live?*
    A. In the White House

60. *How many senators does each state elect?*
    B. 2

61. *Which branch of government writes laws?*
    B. Legislative

62. How many stars are there on the U.S. flag?
    C. 50

63. Which President is referred to as "The Father of our Country"?
    C. George Washington

64. Which country attacked Pearl Harbor during World War II?
    C. Japan

65. Which of the following is not a color on the U.S. flag?
    B. Black

66. Which branch of government meets in the Capitol building?
    B. Legislative

67. How long is one Presidential term?
    B. 4 years

68. What is the name of the first woman Speaker of the House of Representatives?
    A. Nancy Pelosi

69. How many amendments guarantee or address voting rights?
    C. 4

70. What is the name of the highest court in the U.S.?
    B. The Supreme Court

71. Which amendment granted women the right to vote?
D. 19th

72. Who serves as the head of the executive branch of government?
A. The President

73. The President's authority is limited by:
A. The Constitution

74. One of the differences between criminal law and civil law is that:
B. The government cannot be one of the litigants in a civil law case

75. World War II began in what year?
B. 1939

76. John F. Kennedy was assassinated in which city?
C. Dallas, Texas

77. Which of the following states did not attend the Constitutional Convention in May of 1787?
D. Rhode Island

78. Name one of the purposes of the United Nations.
A. For countries to discuss and try to resolve world problems

79. Who signed the Emancipation Proclamation?
C. Abraham Lincoln

80. How many Supreme Court justices are there?
    B. 9

81. Who acts as President of the Senate?
    C. The Vice President of the U.S.

82. Can the U.S. Constitution be changed or amended?
    A. Yes

83. Who selects Supreme Court justices?
    C. The President

83. Which month do Americans vote for President?
    D. November

84. In which month is the new President inaugurated?
    A. January

85. What are the first 10 amendments to the Constitution called?
    B. The Bill of Rights

86. Which USCIS form is used to apply to become a naturalized citizen?
    C. N-400 "Application for Naturalization"

87. Which of the following songs is the U.S. national anthem?
    A. "The Star-Spangled Banner"

88. Who is the Commander in Chief of the U.S. military?
C. The President

89. Which of the following is considered part of the judicial branch of the U.S. government?
B. The Supreme Court

90. What kind of government does the U.S. have?
A. A republic

91. What is the minimum voting age in the U.S.?
B. 18

92. Which of the following is a duty of Congress?
A. To make laws

93. In which year was the Constitution written?
C. 1787

94. What is the most important right granted to U.S. citizens?
B. The right to vote

95. Who were our enemies during World War II?
D. Germany, Italy, and Japan

96. What is the executive of a city government called?
C. Mayor

97. Which of the following amendments pertains to voting?

    C. The 15th Amendment

98. Freedom of speech is mentioned in which of the following documents:

    A. The Bill of Rights

99. Who signs a bill into a law?

    C. The President

100. Which of the following is a ship that brought the Pilgrims to the U.S.?

    C. The Mayflower

★ BIBLIOGRAPHY ★

Gania, Edwin T. (2006). *U.S. Immigration: Step by Step*. 3rd ed. Sphinx Publishing, Naperville, Illinois.

Heller, Stephen and Sicard, Cheri (2003). *U.S. Citizenship for Dummies*. Wiley Publishing Company, Indianapolis, Indiana.

Swick, Edward (2005). *U.S. Citizenship Test: Cliff's Test Prep*. Wiley Publishing Inc., Hoboken, New Jersey.

Wernick, Allan (2004). *U.S. Immigration and Citizenship: Your Complete Guide*. Emmis Books, Cincinnati, Ohio

https:// www.uscis.gov

www.state.gov

★ AMERICAN FACT: *DECLARATION OF INDEPENDENCE* ★

The United States Declaration of Independence is a statement adopted by the Continental Congress on July 4, 1776, announcing that the thirteen American colonies then at war with Great Britain were no longer a part of the British Empire. Written primarily by Thomas Jefferson, the Declaration is a formal explanation of why Congress had voted to declare independence from Great Britain, more than a year after the outbreak of the American Revolutionary War. The birthday of the United States of America—Independence Day—is celebrated on July 4, the day the wording of the Declaration was approved by Congress. After approving the wording on July 4, Congress issued the Declaration of Independence in several forms. It was initially published as a printed broadside that was widely distributed and read to the public. The most famous version of the Declaration, a signed copy that is usually regarded as the Declaration of Independence, is on display at the National Archives in Washington, D.C.

Source: http://en.wikipedia.org/wiki/Declaration_of_American_
Independence

★ AUTHOR BIOGRAPHY ★

Anita Lambert Biase is a former teacher and now works as a freelance writer. She has written and published many stories, poems, articles, and columns in national, regional, and online publications. Anita has also helped to write and edit several collections of educational materials. She recently contributed a story to *Chicken Soup for the Souls of Mothers and Sons* (2006).

Ms. Biase resides in Chula Vista, California, in a community of immigrants and proud new citizens. During her teaching career she taught many students who were new to the United States. She was privileged to be able to watch these children grow and to see them and their families become U.S. citizens.

"Those who doubt the wisdom of the Lady of Liberty need only to go into a second-grade classroom in the early morning. When they hear 30 snaggle-toothed second graders from all over the globe belt out the chorus of 'This Land is My Land,' their reservations will dissolve before the tears can dry on their faces."

—Anita Lambert Biase

POSTSCRIPT BY AUTHOR

Like many Americans, I have always taken my U.S. citizenship as a matter of course, and have never thought much about it. After writing this book and seeing the difficult and lengthy naturalization process firsthand, I will never again take my citizenship for granted.

★ GLOSSARY ★

Acquired Citizenship - Citizenship conferred at birth on children born abroad to a U.S.-citizen parent(s).

Agricultural Worker - As a nonimmigrant class of admission, an alien coming temporarily to the United States to perform agricultural labor or services, as defined by the Secretary of Labor.

Alien - Any person not a citizen or national of the United States.

Amerasian (Vietnam) - Immigrant visas are issued to Amerasians under Public Law 100-202 (Act of 12/22/87), which provides for the admission of aliens born in Vietnam after January 1, 1962 and before January 1, 1976, if the alien was fathered by a U.S. citizen. Spouses, children, and parents or guardians may accompany the alien.

Amerasian Act - Public Law 97-359 (Act of 10/22/82) provides for the immigration to the United States of certain Amerasian children. In order to qualify for benefits under this law, an alien must have been born in Cambodia, Korea,

Laos, Thailand, or Vietnam after December 31, 1950 and before October 22, 1982, and have been fathered by a U.S. citizen.

Application Support Centers - USCIS offers process of biometric service for applicants for immigration benefits. USCIS applications, such as the Application for Naturalization or the Application to Register Permanent Residence or Adjust Status, require the USCIS to conduct an FBI fingerprint background check on the applicant. Applicants will be scheduled to appear at a specific Application Support Center (ASC).

Apprehension - The arrest of a removable alien by U.S. Immigration and Customs Enforcement (ICE). Each apprehension of the same alien in a fiscal year is counted separately.

Asylee - An alien in the United States or at a port of entry who is found to be unable or unwilling to return to his or her country of nationality, or to seek the protection of that country because of persecution or a well-founded fear of persecution. Persecution or the fear thereof must be based on the alien's race, religion, nationality, membership in a particular social group, or political opinion. For persons with no nationality, the country of nationality is considered to be the country in which the alien last habitually resided. Asylees are eligible to adjust to lawful permanent resident status after one year of continuous presence in the United States. These immigrants are limited to 10,000 adjustments per fiscal year.

Beneficiaries - Aliens on whose behalf a U.S. citizen, legal permanent resident, or employer has filed a petition for such aliens to receive immigration benefits from the U.S. Citizenship and Immigration Services. Beneficiaries generally receive a lawful status as a result of their relationship to a U.S. citizen, lawful permanent resident, or U.S. employer.

Border Crosser - An alien resident of the United States re-entering the country after an absence of less than six months in Canada or Mexico, or a nonresident alien entering the United States across the Canadian border for stays of no more than six months or across the Mexican border for stays of no more than 72 hours.

Business Nonimmigrant - An alien coming temporarily to the United States to engage in commercial transactions which do not involve gainful employment in the United States, i.e., engaged in international commerce on behalf of a foreign firm, not employed in the U.S. labor market, and receives no salary from U.S. sources.

Cancellation of Removal - A discretionary benefit adjusting an alien's status from that of deportable alien to one lawfully admitted for permanent residence. Application for cancellation of removal is made during the course of a hearing before an immigration judge.

Certificate of Citizenship - Identity document proving U.S. citizenship. Certificates of citizenship are issued to derivative citizens and to persons who acquired U.S. citizenship (see definitions for Acquired and Derivative

Citizenship).

Child - Generally, an unmarried person under 21 years of age who is: a child born in wedlock; a stepchild, provided that the child was under 18 years of age at the time that the marriage creating the stepchild relationship occurred; a legitimated child, provided that the child was legitimated while in the legal custody of the legitimating parent; a child born out of wedlock, when a benefit is sought on the basis of its relationship with its mother, or to its father if the father has or had a bona fide relationship with the child; a child adopted while under 16 years of age who has resided since adoption in the legal custody of the adopting parents for at least two years; or an orphan, under 16 years of age, who has been adopted abroad by a U.S. citizen or has an immediate-relative visa petition submitted in his/her behalf and is coming to the United States for adoption by a U.S. citizen.

Civil Surgeon - A medically trained, licensed and experienced doctor practicing in the U.S. who is certified by USCIS (U.S. Citizenship and Immigration Service). These medical professionals receive U.S. immigration-focused training in order to provide examinations as required by the CDC (Center for Disease Control and Prevention) and USCIS. For medical examinations given overseas, please see Panel Physician.

> **IMPORTANT:** medical examinations will not be recognized if they are given by a doctor in the U.S. who is not a Civil Surgeon; please make sure that your appointment is with a Civil Surgeon or your

results and documents will be invalid.

Conditional Resident - Any alien granted permanent resident status on a conditional basis (e.g., a spouse of a U.S. citizen; an immigrant investor), who is required to petition for the removal of the set conditions before the second anniversary of the approval of his or her conditional status.

Country of -

Birth: The country in which a person is born.

Chargeability: The independent country to which an immigrant entering under the preference system is accredited for purposes of numerical limitations.

Citizenship: The country in which a person is born (and has not renounced or lost citizenship) or naturalized and to which that person owes allegiance and by which he or she is entitled to be protected.

Former Allegiance: The previous country of citizenship of a naturalized U.S. citizen or of a person who derived U.S. citizenship.

(Last) Residence: The country in which an alien habitually resided prior to entering the United States.

Nationality: The country of a person's citizenship or

country in which the person is deemed a national.

Crewman - A foreign national serving in a capacity required for normal operations and service on board a vessel or aircraft. Crewmen are admitted for twenty-nine days, with no extensions. Two categories of crewmen are defined in the INA: D1, departing from the United States with the vessel or aircraft on which he arrived or some other vessel or aircraft; and D2, departing from Guam with the vessel on which he arrived.

Cuban/Haitian Entrant - Status accorded to 1) Cubans who entered illegally or were paroled into the United States between April 15, 1980, and October 10, 1980, and 2) Haitians who entered illegally or were paroled into the country before January 1, 1981. Cubans and Haitians meeting these criteria who have continuously resided in the United States since before January 1, 1982, and who were known to Immigration before that date, may adjust to permanent residence under a provision of the Immigration Control and Reform Act of 1986.

Deportable Alien - An alien in and admitted to the United States subject to any grounds of removal specified in the Immigration and Nationality Act. This includes any alien illegally in the United States, regardless of whether the alien entered the country by fraud or misrepresentation or entered legally but subsequently violated the terms of his or her nonimmigrant classification or status.

Deportation - The formal removal of an alien from the

United States when the alien has been found removable for violating the immigration laws. Deportation is ordered by an immigration judge without any punishment being imposed or contemplated. Prior to April 1997 deportation and exclusion were separate removal procedures. The Illegal Immigration Reform and Immigrant Responsibility Act of 1996 consolidated these procedures. After April 1, 1997, aliens in and admitted to the United States may be subject to removal based on deportability. Now called removal, this function is managed by U.S. Immigration and Customs Enforcement.

Derivative Citizenship - Citizenship conveyed to children through the naturalization of parents or, under certain circumstances, to foreign-born children adopted by U.S.-citizen parents, provided certain conditions are met.

District - Geographic areas into which the United States and its territories are divided for the USCIS's field operations, or one of three overseas offices located in Rome, Bangkok, and Mexico City. Each district office, headed by a district director, has a specified service area that may include part of a state, an entire state, or many states. District offices are where most USCIS field staff are located. District offices are responsible for providing certain immigration services and benefits to people resident in their service area, and for enforcing immigration laws in that jurisdiction. Certain applications are filed directly with district offices, many kinds of interviews are conducted at these offices, and USCIS staff is available to answer questions, provide forms, and provide assistance.

Diversity - A category of immigrants replacing the earlier categories for nationals of underrepresented countries and countries adversely "affected" by the Immigration and Nationality Act Amendments of 1965 (P.L. 89-236). The annual limit on diversity immigration was 40,000 during fiscal years 1992-1994, under a transitional diversity program, and 55,000 beginning in fiscal year 1995, under a permanent diversity program.

Docket Control - The DHS mechanism for tracking the case status of potentially removable aliens.

Employer Sanctions - The employer sanctions provision of the Immigration Reform and Control Act of 1986 prohibits employers from hiring, recruiting, or referring for a fee aliens known to be unauthorized to work in the United States. Violators of the law are subject to a series of civil fines for violations or criminal penalties when there is a pattern or practice of violations.

Exchange Visitor - An alien coming temporarily to the United States as a participant in a program approved by the secretary of state for the purpose of teaching, instructing or lecturing, studying, observing, conducting research, consulting, demonstrating special skills, or receiving training.

Exclusion - Prior to the Illegal Immigration Reform and Immigrant Responsibility Act of 1996, exclusion was the formal term for denial of an alien's entry into the United States. The decision to exclude an alien was made by an immigration judge after an exclusion hearing. Since April 1,

1997, the process of adjudicating inadmissibility may take place in either an expedited removal process or in removal proceedings before an immigration judge.

Fiancé(e)s of U.S. Citizen - A nonimmigrant alien coming to the United States to conclude a valid marriage with a U.S. citizen within ninety days after entry.

Field Offices - Offices found in some districts that serve a portion of the district's jurisdiction. A field office, headed by an officer-in-charge, provides many services and enforcement functions. Their locations are determined, in part, to increase convenience to USCIS's customers.

Files Control Office - An USCIS field office — either a district (including USCIS overseas offices) or a suboffice of that district — where alien case files are maintained and controlled.

Fiscal Year - Currently, the twelve-month period beginning October 1 and ending September 30. Historically, until 1831 and from 1843-1849, the twelve-month period ending September 30 of the respective year; from 1832-1842 and 1850-1867, ending December 31 of the respective year; from 1868-1976, ending June 30 of the respective year. The transition quarter (TQ) for 1976 covers the three-month period, July-September 1976.

Foreign Government Official - As a nonimmigrant class of admission, an alien coming temporarily to the United States who has been accredited by a foreign government to function as an ambassador, public minister, career diplomatic or consular officer, other accredited official, or an attendant, servant, or personal employee of an accredited official, and all above aliens' spouses and unmarried minor (or dependent) children.

Foreign Information Media Representative - As a nonimmigrant class of admission, an alien coming temporarily to the United States as a bona fide representative of foreign press, radio, film, or other foreign information media and the alien's spouse and unmarried minor (or dependent) children.

Foreign State of Chargeability - The independent country to which an immigrant entering under the preference system is accredited. No more than 7 percent of the family-sponsored and employment-based visas may be issued to natives of any one independent country in a fiscal year. No one dependency of any independent country may receive more than 2 percent of the family-sponsored and employment-based visas issued. Since these limits are based on visa issuance rather than entries into the United States, and immigrant visas are valid for six months, there is not total correspondence between these two occurrences. Chargeability is usually determined by country of birth. Exceptions are made to prevent the separation of family members when the limitation for the country of birth has been met.

General Naturalization Provisions - The basic requirements for naturalization that every applicant must meet, unless a member of a special class. General provisions require an applicant to be at least 18 years of age and a lawful permanent resident with five years of continuous residence in the United States, have been physically present in the country for half that period, and have established good moral character for at least that period.

Geographic Area of Chargeability - Any one of five geographic regions — Africa, East Asia, Latin America and the Caribbean, Near East and South Asia, and the former Soviet Union and Eastern Europe — into which the world is divided for the initial admission of refugees to the United States. Annual consultations between the executive branch and the Congress determine the ceiling on the number of refugees who can be admitted to the United States from each area. Beginning in fiscal year 1987, an unallocated reserve was incorporated into the admission ceilings.

Hemispheric Ceilings - Statutory limits on immigration to the United States in effect from 1968 to October 1978. Mandated by the Immigration and Nationality Act Amendments of 1965, the ceiling on immigration from the Eastern Hemisphere was set at 170,000, with a per-country limit of 20,000. Immigration from the Western Hemisphere was held to 120,000, without a per-country limit until January 1, 1977. The Western Hemisphere was then made subject to a 20,000 per-country limit. Effective October 1978, the separate hemisphere limits were abolished in favor of a worldwide limit.

Immediate Relatives - Certain immigrants who, because of their close relationship to U.S. citizens, are exempt from the numerical limitations imposed on immigration to the

United States. Immediate relatives are: spouses of citizens, children (under 21 years of age and unmarried) of citizens, and parents of citizens 21 years of age or older.

Immigration Act of 1990 - Public Law 101-649 (Act of November 29, 1990), which increased the limits on legal immigration to the United States, revised all grounds for exclusion and deportation, authorized temporary protected status to aliens of designated countries, revised and established new nonimmigrant admission categories, revised and extended the Visa Waiver Pilot Program, and revised naturalization authority and requirements.

Immigration and Nationality Act - The Act (INA) which, along with other immigration laws, treaties, and conventions of the United States, relates to the immigration, temporary admission, naturalization, and removal of aliens.

Immigration Judge - An attorney appointed by the attorney general to act as an administrative judge within the Executive Office for Immigration Review. He or she is qualified to conduct specified classes of proceedings, including removal proceedings.

Immigration Marriage Fraud Amendments of 1986 - Public Law 99-639 (Act of 11/10/86), which was passed in order to deter immigration-related marriage fraud. Its major provision stipulates that aliens deriving their immigrant status based on a marriage of less than two years are conditional immigrants. To remove their conditional status, the immigrants must apply at a U.S. Citizenship and Immigration Services office during the 90-day period before their second-year anniversary of receiving conditional status. If the alien cannot show that the marriage through which the status was obtained was and is a valid one, the conditional immigrant status may be terminated and they may become deportable.

Immigration Reform and Control Act of 1986 (IRCA) - Public Law 99-603 (Act of 11/6/86), which was passed in order to control and deter illegal immigration to the United States. Its major provisions stipulate legalization of undocumented aliens who had been continuously unlawfully present since 1982, legalization of certain agricultural workers, sanctions for employers who knowingly hire undocumented workers, and increased enforcement at U.S. borders.

Inadmissible - An alien seeking admission at a port of entry who does not meet the criteria in the INA for admission. The alien may be placed in removal proceedings or, under certain circumstances, allowed to withdraw his or her application for admission.

International Representative - As a nonimmigrant class of admission, an alien coming temporarily to the United States as a principal or other accredited representative of a foreign government (whether officially recognized or not recognized by the United States) to an international organization, an international organization officer or employee, and all above aliens' spouses and unmarried minor (or dependent) children.

Intracompany Trainee - An alien, employed for at least one

★ *Your U.S. Citizenship Guide* ★

continuous year out of the last three by an international firm or corporation, who seeks to enter the United States temporarily in order to continue to work for the same employer, or a subsidiary or affiliate, in a capacity that is primarily managerial, executive, or involves specialized knowledge, and the alien's spouse and minor unmarried children.

Labor Certification - Requirement for U.S. employers seeking to employ certain persons whose immigration to the United States is based on job skills or nonimmigrant temporary workers coming to perform services for which qualified authorized workers are unavailable in the United States. Labor certification is issued by the secretary of labor and contains attestations by U.S. employers as to the numbers of U.S. workers available to undertake the employment sought by an applicant, and the effect of the alien's employment on the wages and working conditions of U.S. workers similarly employed. Determination of labor availability in the United States is made at the time of a visa application and at the location where the applicant wishes to work.

Lawful Permanent Resident (LPR) - Any person not a citizen of the United States who is residing in the United States under legally recognized and lawfully recorded permanent residence as an immigrant. Also known as "permanent resident alien," "resident alien permit holder," and "green card holder."

Legalization Dependents - A maximum of 55,000 visas were issued to spouses and children of aliens legalized under the provisions of the Immigration Reform and Control Act of 1986 in each of fiscal years 1992-1994.

Legalized Aliens - Certain illegal aliens who were eligible to apply for temporary resident status under the legalization provision of the Immigration Reform and Control Act of 1986. To be eligible, aliens must have continuously resided in the United States in an unlawful status since January 1, 1982, not be excludable, and have entered the United States either 1) illegally before January 1, 1982, or 2) as temporary visitors before January 1, 1982, with their authorized stay expiring before that date or with the government's knowledge of their unlawful status before that date. Legalization consists of two stages: temporary and then permanent residency. In order to adjust to permanent status, aliens must have had continuous residence in the United States, be admissible as an immigrant, and demonstrate at least a minimal understanding and knowledge of the English language and U.S. history and government.

Legitimated - Most countries have legal procedures for natural fathers of children born out of wedlock to acknowledge their children. A legitimated child from any country has two legal parents and cannot qualify as an orphan unless: 1) only one of the parents is living, or 2) both of the parents have abandoned the child.

Medical Waiver - A medical waiver permits an immigration applicant to be allowed into or remain in the United States despite having a health condition identified as grounds of inadmissibility. Terms and conditions can be applied to a medical waiver on a case-by-case basis.

Migrant - A person who leaves his of her country of origin to seek residence in another country.

Naturalization - The conferring, by any means, of citizenship upon a person after birth.

North American Free Trade Agreement (NAFTA) - Public Law 103-182 (Act of 12/8/93), superseded the United States-Canada Free-Trade Agreement as of 1/1/94. It continues the special, reciprocal trading relationship between the United States and Canada (see United States-Canada Free-Trade Agreement), and establishes a similar relationship with Mexico.

Nursing Relief Act of 1989 - Public Law 101-238 (Act of 12/18/89), provides for the adjustment to permanent resident status of certain nonimmigrants who, as of September 1, 1989, had H-1 nonimmigrant status as registered nurses, who had been employed in that capacity for at least three years, and whose continued nursing employment meets certain labor certification requirements.

Orphan - The Immigration and Nationality Act provides a definition of an orphan for the purposes of immigration to the United States.

A child may be considered an orphan because of the death or disappearance of, abandonment or desertion by, or separation or loss from both parents. The child of an unwed mother or surviving parent may be considered an orphan if that parent is unable to care for the child properly and has, in writing, irrevocably released the child for emigration and adoption. The child of an unwed mother may be considered an orphan, as long as the mother does not marry (which would result in the child's having a stepfather) and as long as the child's biological father has not legitimated the child. If the father legitimates the child or the mother marries, the mother is no longer considered a sole parent. The child of a surviving parent may also be an orphan if the surviving parent has not married since the death of the other parent (which would result in the child's having a stepfather or stepmother). Note: Prospective adoptive parents should be sure that a child fits the definition of "orphan" before adopting a child from another country, because not all children adopted abroad meet the definition of "orphan," and therefore may not be eligible to immigrate to the United States.

Parolee - A parolee is an alien, appearing to be inadmissible to the inspecting officer, allowed into the United States for urgent humanitarian reasons or when that alien's entry is determined to be for significant public benefit. Parole does not constitute a formal admission to the United States and confers temporary status only, requiring parolees to leave when the conditions supporting their parole cease to exist. Types of parolees include:

> **Deferred inspection:** authorized at the port upon an alien's arrival; may be conferred by an immigration inspector when aliens appear at a port of entry with documentation, but after preliminary examination, some question remains about their admissibility

which can best be answered at their point of destination.

Advance parole: authorized at a USCIS district office in advance of an alien's arrival; may be issued to aliens residing in the United States in other than lawful permanent resident status, who have an unexpected need to travel and return, and whose conditions of stay do not otherwise allow for readmission to the United States if they depart.

Port-of-entry parole: authorized at the port upon alien's arrival; applies to a wide variety of situations and is used at the discretion of the supervisory immigration inspector, usually to allow short periods of entry. Examples include allowing aliens who could not be issued the necessary documentation within the required time period, or who were otherwise inadmissible, to attend a funeral and permitting the entry of emergency workers, such as firefighters, to assist with an emergency.

Humanitarian parole: authorized at USCIS headquarters or overseas district offices for "urgent humanitarian reasons" specified in the law. It is used in cases of medical emergency and comparable situations.

Significant public benefit parole: authorized at USCIS headquarters' Office of International Affairs for "significant public benefit" specified in the law.

It is generally used for aliens who enter to take part in legal proceedings when there is a benefit to the government. These requests must be submitted by a law enforcement agency.

Overseas parole: authorized at a USCIS district or suboffice while the alien is still overseas; designed to constitute long-term admission to the United States. In recent years, most of the aliens USCIS has processed through overseas parole have arrived under special legislation or international migration agreements.

Permanent Resident - Any person not a citizen of the United States who is residing in the U.S. under legally recognized and lawfully recorded permanent residence as an immigrant. Also known as "permanent resident alien," "lawful permanent resident," "resident alien permit holder," and "green card holder."

Port of Entry - Any location in the United States or its territories that is designated as a point of entry for aliens and U.S. citizens. All district and files control offices are also considered ports, since they become locations of entry for aliens adjusting to immigrant status.

Refugee - Any person who is outside his or her country of nationality who is unable or unwilling to return to that country because of persecution or a well-founded fear of persecution. Persecution or the fear thereof must be based on the alien's race, religion, nationality, membership in a particular social group, or political opinion. People with no nationality must generally be outside their country of last habitual residence to qualify as a refugee. Refugees are subject to ceilings by geographic area set annually by the president in consultation with Congress and are eligible to adjust to lawful permanent resident status after one year of continuous presence in the United States.

Registry Date - Aliens who have continuously resided in the United States since January 1, 1972, are of good moral character, and are not inadmissible, are eligible to adjust to legal permanent resident status under the registry provision. Before the Immigration Reform and Control Act of 1986 amended the date, aliens had to have been in the country continuously since June 30, 1948 to qualify.

Resident Alien - Applies to non-U.S. citizens currently residing in the United States. The term is applied in three different manners; please see Permanent Resident, Conditional Resident, and Returning Resident.

Returning Resident - Any lawful permanent resident who has been outside the United States and is returning to the U.S. Also defined as a "special immigrant." If outside of the U.S. for more than 180 days, he or she must apply for readmission to the United States. If outside of the U.S. for more than one year and is returning to his or her permanent residence in the United States, he or she usually must have re-entry documentation from USCIS or an immigrant visa from the Department of State.

Safe Haven - Temporary refuge, given to migrants who have fled their countries of origin to seek protection or relief from persecution or other hardships, until they can return to their countries safely or, if necessary, until they can obtain permanent relief from the conditions they fled.

Special Immigrants - Certain categories of immigrants who were exempt from numerical limitation before fiscal year 1992 and subject to limitation under the employment-based fourth preference beginning in 1992; persons who lost citizenship by marriage; persons who lost citizenship by serving in foreign armed forces; ministers of religion and other religious workers, their spouses and children; certain employees and former employees of the U.S. government abroad, their spouses and children; Panama Canal Act immigrants; certain foreign medical school graduates, their spouses and children; certain retired employees of international organizations, their spouses and children; juvenile court dependents; and certain aliens serving in the U.S. armed forces, along with their spouses and children.

Stowaway - An alien coming to the United States surreptitiously on an airplane or vessel without legal status of admission. Such an alien is subject to denial of formal admission and return to the point of embarkation by the transportation carrier.

Student - As a nonimmigrant class of admission, an alien coming temporarily to the United States to pursue a full course of study in an approved program in either an academic (college, university, seminary, conservatory, academic high school, elementary school, other institution, or language training program) or a vocational or other recognized nonacademic institution.

Transit Alien - An alien in immediate and continuous transit through the United States, with or without a visa, including 1) aliens who qualify as persons entitled to pass in transit to and from the United Nations Headquarters District and foreign countries, and 2) foreign government officials and their spouses and unmarried minor (or dependent) children in transit.

Transit Without Visa (TWOV) - A transit alien traveling without a nonimmigrant visa under section 233 of the INA. An alien admitted under agreements with a transportation line, which guarantees his immediate and continuous passage to a foreign destination.

Underrepresented Countries, Natives of - The Immigration Amendments of 1988, Public Law 101-658 (Act of 11/5/88), allowed for 10,000 visas to be issued to natives of underrepresented countries in each of fiscal years 1990 and 1991. Underrepresented countries are countries that received less than 25 percent of the maximum allowed under the country limitations (20,000 for independent countries and 5,000 for dependencies) in fiscal year 1988.

United States - Canada Free-Trade Agreement - Public Law 100-449 (Act of 9/28/88) established a special, reciprocal trading relationship between the United States and Canada. It provided two new classes of nonimmigrant admission for temporary visitors to the United States:

Canadian-citizen businesspersons and their spouses and unmarried minor children. Entry is facilitated for visitors seeking classification as visitors for business, treaty traders or investors, intracompany transferees, or other business people engaging in activities at a professional level. Such visitors are not required to obtain nonimmigrant visas, prior petitions, labor certifications, or prior approval, but must satisfy the inspecting officer that they are seeking entry to engage in activities at a professional level and that they are so qualified. The United States-Canada Free-Trade Agreement was superseded by the North American Free-Trade Agreement (NAFTA) as of 1/1/94.

Visa - A U.S. visa allows the bearer to apply for entry to the U.S. in a certain classification, e.g., student (F), visitor (B), temporary worker (H). A visa does not grant the bearer the right to enter the United States. The Department of State (DOS) is responsible for visa adjudication at U.S. embassies and consulates outside of the United States. The Department of Homeland Security (DHS) Bureau of Customs and Border Protection (BCBP) immigration inspectors determine admission into, length of stay, and conditions of stay in the U.S. at a port of entry. The information on a nonimmigrant visa only relates to when an individual may apply for entry into the U.S. DHS immigration inspectors will record the terms of your admission on your Arrival/Departure Record (I-94 white or I-94W green) and in your passport.

Visa Waiver Program - Allows citizens of certain selected countries, traveling temporarily to the United States under the nonimmigrant admission classes of visitors for pleasure and visitors for business, to enter the United States without obtaining nonimmigrant visas. Admission is for no more than 90 days. The program was instituted by the Immigration Reform and Control Act of 1986 (entries began 7/1/88). Under the Guam Visa Waiver Program, certain visitors from designated countries may visit Guam only for up to 15 days without first having to obtain nonimmigrant visitor visas.

Voluntary Departure - The departure of an alien from the United States without an order of removal. The departure may or may not have been preceded by a hearing before an immigration judge. An alien allowed to voluntarily depart concedes removability but does not have a bar to seeking admission at a port of entry at any time. Failure to depart within the time granted results in a fine and a ten-year bar to several forms of relief from deportation.

Withdrawal - An arriving alien's voluntary retraction of an application for admission to the United States in lieu of a removal hearing before an immigration judge or an expedited removal.

★ INDEX ★

A

Adjudication 56

Adjustment 57, 58

Administration 21, 22

Age 45

Agencies 85, 86, 91

Alien 67, 70, 76, 77

Allegiance 32, 35, 38, 43, 44

Amendment 26, 154, 167

Amendments 41, 113

America 99, 109, 110, 129, 133, 135, 138, 141, 142, 170

American 45, 52

Application 32, 33, 38-44, 46, 48, 50, 51, 56, 58, 65, 67, 70, 73, 76, 82, 85, 89-91, 95-97, 99, 101, 105, 176, 182, 183, 186-191

Approval 43, 59

Assistance 79, 80, 85

Asylum 22-34, 62, 77, 81, 82

Availability 57

B

Beneficiary 46, 68, 71, 79

Benefits 59, 63, 78-80

Birth 16, 24, 27, 33, 39, 43, 45

C

Campaign 121, 135

Category 66, 69

Certificate 43, 44

Challenge 99

Character 45, 47, 48

Children 60, 61, 68, 72, 74, 79, 80

Child Support 48

Citizen 16, 17, 21, 22, 24, 27,
    28, 31-35, 37, 38, 42, 45-
    48, 51-53, 55-57, 59-61,
    63, 64, 66, 99, 100, 101,
    103-105, 118, 142, 177,
    159, 170, 176, 177, 179,
    181-184, 187-189

Citizenship 38, 39, 41, 43, 45,
    46, 47, 50

Community Service 48

Complicated 15, 16

Comprehension 100, 101, 140

Condition 43

Congress 78, 79, 83, 85, 111,
    114-118, 121, 122, 124,
    125, 129, 130, 133, 139,
    141, 144-146, 152, 153,
    155, 159, 167, 169, 171

Constitution 17, 25, 26, 38, 41,
    42, 44, 45, 50, 112, 113,
    114, 116, 118, 143, 144,
    153, 145, 146, 147, 148,
    149, 152, 153, 154, 156,
    157, 158, 159, 163, 164,
    167, 171, 172, 173

Controlled Substance 49

Conviction 48

Country 49, 52, 53

Court 49, 109, 117, 128

Crime 49

Criminal 79

D

Democracy 113, 144

Designation 78, 79

Division 21, 24

Documents 40, 42, 90

Dress 103

Drugs 48

Dual Citizenship 34

E

Election 120, 123, 126, 142

Eligibility 16, 17, 55, 58, 77, 81,
    82

Employer 56, 61

Employment 59, 61

EMployment 63, 68, 70

English 38, 42-45, 99-102, 106,
    137, 138-140, 142

Equal 148

F

Family 59, 63, 64, 66

Fee 89-91, 96

Fees 40, 73, 84, 91, 96, 97

Felony 49

Fingerprint 89, 96

Form 65, 67, 68, 70, 76, 81, 84, 85

Form N-400 89, 91, 99, 103

Forms 99

Freedom 138

G

Government 21, 25, 26, 27, 28, 29, 30, 31, 38, 41, 43, 45, 52, 83, 86, 99, 100, 102, 109, 112-121, 125, 130, 136-138, 143, 144, 146-149, 153, 156-159, 161, 162, 164-168, 171, 172, 176, 180, 182, 188, 189, 191, 192

Green Card 46, 49, 53, 55, 56, 57, 58, 59, 60, 61, 89, 96, 103, 180, 181, 183

H

Hearing 44

History 38, 39, 41, 42, 45, 99, 102, 106, 109, 123, 128, 130, 133, 135, 137

Homeland Security 78, 79, 84, 86

I

Immigrant 22, 34, 37, 56, 57

Immigration 15, 21-24, 32, 40, 56, 62-64, 71, 77-80, 82, 84, 90, 99, 151

Independence 111, 113, 122, 128, 141

Information 93, 94

Institution 49, 52

Instructions 89, 91

International 22-24

Interview 39, 42-44, 99, 100-106, 137

Inteview 99-106

Investment 59, 61, 74-76

J

Job 68

Jurisdiction 40

Justice 25

K

Knowledge 41, 43, 45, 152

L

Language 137, 139, 140, 142

Law 49, 62, 145, 146, 148, 153, 164, 168, 173, 187, 189, 190

Laws 25-29, 33-35, 44, 50, 53, 117, 118, 132, 133

Legal 46

Legislature 144

Liberty 24-26, 141, 158

License 43, 52

Location 41, 42

Lottery 62

Loyalty 49

M

Maintain 79

Marriage 43, 47, 59, 63, 66, 94

Medicare 52

Military 39, 41, 51

Moral Character 47

N

Native 23, 32, 35

Naturalization 15, 16, 21, 22, 31-38, 40, 41, 43, 44, 55, 89, 90, 92-94, 137, 142, 178, 180-188, 191

Nerves 106

Notice 42, 44

O

Oath 17, 44, 142

Oath of Allegiance 44

Obey 53

Organization 52, 123

P

Paperwork 99, 103, 104

Parent 59, 60, 65, 80

Parents 93

Parole 77, 84

Passport 43

Permanent Resident 37, 38, 44, 46, 49-52, 55-57, 59, 64-67, 71, 74, 76, 78, 80, 81, 90

Petition 38, 42, 44, 56-58, 60, 61, 67, 70, 76

Physical Presence 50, 52

Political Party 30

Practice 102

Prepare 102

President 114, 117-128, 130, 131, 133-135, 145, 146, 152, 153, 155-162, 164, 165, 167, 169-173

Principles 44

Privilege 176

Privileges 16, 26, 31, 33

Procedure 37

Process 21, 22, 23, 25-27, 32, 33, 37, 44, 55-57, 68, 70-72, 74, 75, 81

Property 52

Protection 81, 83, 147, 148

Q

Questions 99, 100, 102

R

Read 45, 137, 140

Refugee 22, 23, 24, 77, 81, 82

Regulate 113

Relationship 47, 64, 65

Relative 57, 59

Request 56

Requirement 51, 70, 90, 137

Research 52

Residence 50, 58

Resident 37, 38, 43-46, 49-53, 55-57, 59, 64-67, 71, 74, 76-78, 80, 81, 90, 175-177, 182-185, 187, 191

Responsibilities 53, 142

Responsibility 59

Ressettlement 81-83

Rights 16, 24-27, 33, 35, 141-143, 146-149, 153, 154, 158, 163, 170, 173, 182, 190

S

Security 42, 78, 79, 84, 86, 103

Social Security 52

Speak 137, 138, 140, 142

Spouse 46, 47, 52, 66-68, 72, 74, 80, 94

Status 63, 64, 66, 71, 74, 76-78, 80-84

T

Taxes 48, 53

Territory 45, 52

Test 41, 99, 102, 137, 142, 151, 152

Testimony 49

Transfer 68, 69

Truth 105

U

Understand 102

United States 21, 23, 24, 26-30,

33, 34, 37, 43-45, 49, 50, 52, 53, 55, 57, 58, 63-67, 69-72, 74-79, 81-84, 86, 94, 95, 99, 101, 102, 109, 112, 113, 118-120, 126, 131, 132-136, 141, 142, 143, 145, 152, 153, 158, 159, 161, 164, 168, 178, 183, 184, 188, 189, 191

USCIS 16, 21, 22, 24, 32, 38, 39, 42, 44, 46, 48, 53, 56-58, 89, 91, 93-96, 99, 105

V

Visa 52, 55-59, 61-67, 70-73, 84, 86

Vocabulary 141

Volunteer 48

Vote 26, 27, 30, 128, 130, 132, 141, 148, 167, 170, 172, 176

W

Waiting Lists 57

Work 55